THE
REGENT'S
CANAL

CONWAY
Bloomsbury Publishing Plc
50 Bedford Square, London, WC1B 3DP, UK
29 Earlsfort Terrace, Dublin 2, Ireland

BLOOMSBURY, CONWAY and the Conway logo are trademarks of Bloomsbury Publishing Plc

First edition published in 2012 by Frances Lincoln Ltd
This second edition published 2018 by Frances Lincoln Ltd and 2023 by Bloomsbury Publishing Plc

A catalogue record for this book is available from the British Library

Library of Congress Cataloguing-in-Publication data has been applied for

ISBN: PB: 978-1-8448-6693-9; ePub: 978-1-8448-6690-8; ePDF: 978-1-8448-6691-5

2 4 6 8 10 9 7 5 3 1

Typeset in 8/11pt Baskerville by David Fathers
Printed and bound in India by Replika Press Pvt. Ltd.

To find out more about our authors and books visit www.bloomsbury.com and sign up for our newsletters

Note: While every effort has been made to ensure the accuracy of this guidebook, changes can occur over time. If you discover any important changes to the routes in this book, we're happy to hear about them.
Please email us at conway@bloomsbury.com with any comments.

THE REGENT'S CANAL

An Urban Towpath Route
from Little Venice to the Olympic Park

Written & illustrated by
DAVID FATHERS

CONWAY
LONDON · OXFORD · NEW YORK · NEW DELHI · SYDNEY

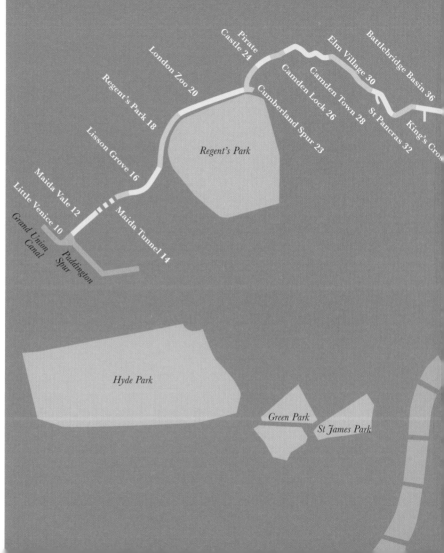

THE REGENT'S CANAL
CONTENTS

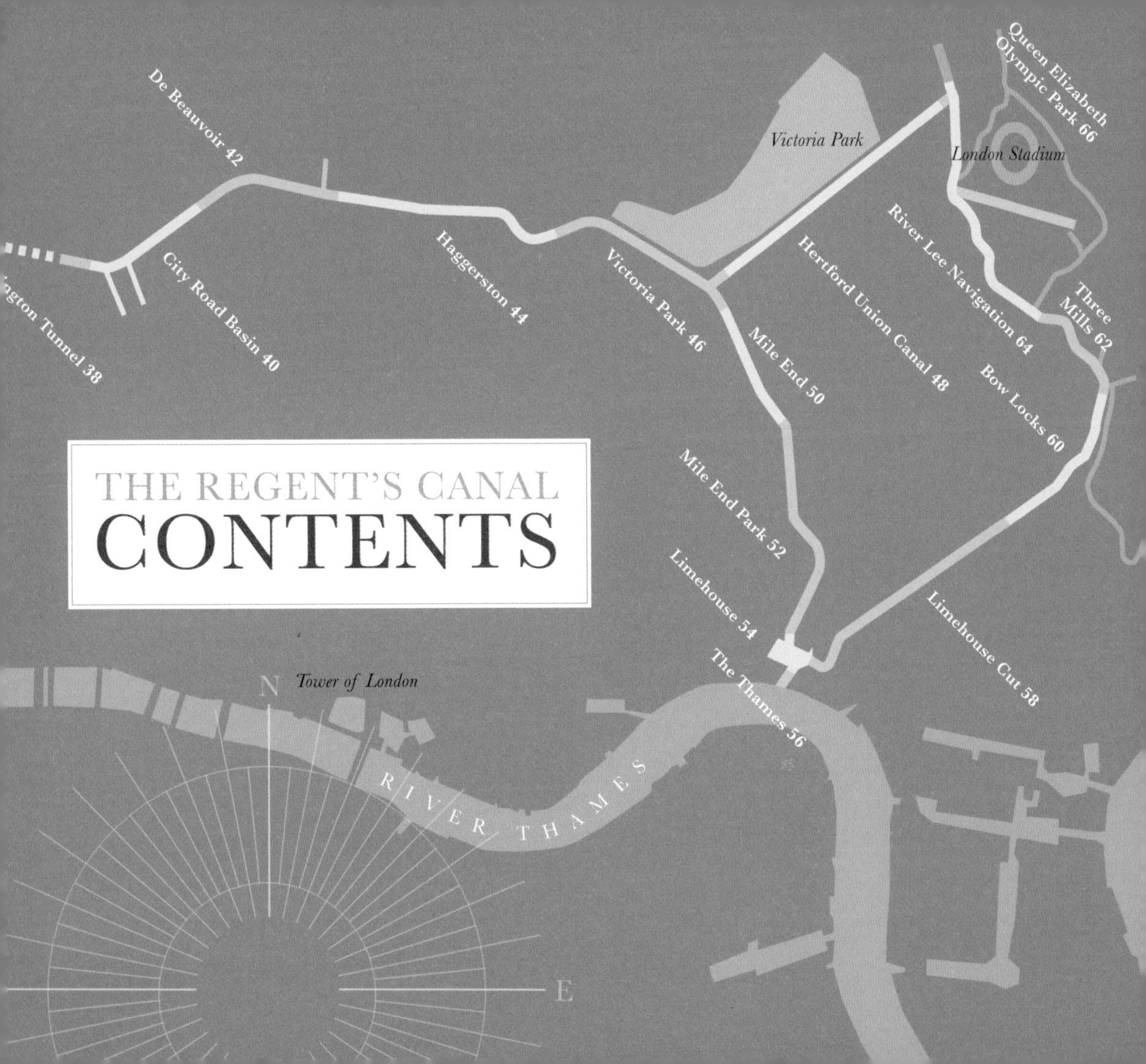

Victoria Park

London Stadium

Tower of London

RIVER THAMES

N

E

For Sheila, Florence & Alex

INTRODUCTION

This book is a guide to and celebration of four man-made waterways in London: the Regent's Canal, the Hertford Union Canal, the Limehouse Cut and the River Lee Navigation. In 1929, the Regent's Canal became part of the Grand Union Canal. Although officially known by this name, it is still commonly referred to as the Regent's Canal, and many maps and signposts refer to it as such. As the most iconic and best known of the London canals, the name persists.

Having lived in London for more than forty years and travelled across the metropolis on foot, bicycle, bus and Tube, I thought I knew the place well. That was until I stepped on to the canal towpath for the first time and saw parts of London from a totally different perspective.

The canal towpaths in this book form an urban foot and cycleway that unites many parts of the best and least known parts of north and east London.

- *From the playing fields of Regent's Park to the Queen Elizabeth Olympic Park in Newham.*
- *From the fine Regency buildings of Little Venice to the twentieth-century social housing in Haggerston.*
- *From the chugging narrowboat of St Pancras Basin gliding into the lock, to the sleek white Eurostar train roaring off to Paris and Brussels.*
- *From the former home of breakfast television – TV:am in Camden – to the Big Breakfast studios by Old Ford Lock.*
- *From the opium dens of squalid nineteenth-century Limehouse – home to the fictional characters of Wilde, Dickens and Ackroyd – to the shiny modern marina and riverside apartments of today.*

The canal towpaths brings contact with an array of contemporary and historical references that surprise, intrigue and fascinate.

WALKING AND CYCLING THE TOWPATHS

In researching and writing this book I travelled the canals from west to east, from Little Venice to the Queen Elizabeth Olympic Park, via the River Thames at Limehouse. Thus the book is laid out in the same fashion.

To walk or cycle the whole 22km route could take several days if you stopped to take in each feature. Each double page is treated as a separate entity and can be explored on its own or with adjacent sections. The nearest Underground and train stations are marked. The scale of the maps is not consistent throughout the book. The distance covered, in metres, is marked on each double-page spread.

Occasionally towpaths are closed for repairs or maintenance. Diversions are usually marked out on maps by the closures. However there are some sections of the towpaths where the access gates have simply not been unlocked. Sometimes towpaths are closed as a result of building work adjacent to the canals. At the time of writing this second edition there are still major building works going on around King's Cross and St Pancras and the Olympic Park. And

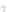

there is an almost endless conversion of old factories and warehouses and the building of new apartments along the canals. Once no one wanted to be close to the polluted and noisome canals; now there is a great clamour for waterside living. Also, since researching the first edition, I've noticed a greater number of narrowboats moored up along the towpaths than ever before (the figure has more than doubled). Given the shortage of affordable housing in London many people are taking to living on the canal as an alternative.

A BRIEF HISTORY

The Regent's Canal was a latecomer in the grand scheme of canal building, opening only five years before the first steam railway.

By contrast, the River Lee Navigation is the oldest canal in the UK, having been developed from the Elizabethan era. Its purpose was to enable barges to move large quantities of goods efficiently from Hertford to London. In 1770. the Limehouse Cut was created to reduce the journey time from the Navigation to Limehouse, by avoiding the Isle of Dogs loop of the River Thames.

Five years earlier, in 1765, the Bridgewater Canal was opened between the Duke of Bridgewater's coalmines in Worsley and Manchester and was the first commercial canal to be built in Britain. Within thirty-five years a large network of canals had been built across the UK, but the closest the system got to London was the Grand Junction Canal, which reached Paddington in 1801.

All barges carrying raw and finished material in and out of London had to transfer loads on to horse drawn wagons. These were then transported along the New Road (now known as Marylebone Road) into London and the City.

By the beginning of the of the nineteenth century there became an urgent need to connect the then Grand Junction Canal to the River Thames at a point where sea-going vessels could dock. Since 1800 a growing number of docks and basins to the east of the city had sprung up.

At the turn of the nineteenth century, Thomas Homer, a barge owner, planned a canal link from the Paddington Spur of the Grand Junction Canal to the Thames at Limehouse, but had few financial resources. The architect and visionary John Nash heard of Homer's plan in 1810 and incorporated it into his plans for Regent's Park. The Regent's Canal Company was formed and work on the canal commenced in 1812. The final link to Limehouse and the River Thames was completed in 1820.

At the time, 90 per cent of the route of the Regent's Canal and the Limehouse Cut was through open countryside, as this was beyond the city boundaries. Many engravings of this period show the canals surrounded by farms and woods. As

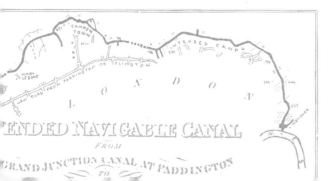

London started to expand rapidly in the nineteenth century, wharfs, warehouse and factories, attracted to the canal's transportation facilities, soon sprang up along the banks, and the canal's character began to evolve.

By the 1840s, the growth of the railway system was well under way. Despite this, the amount of tonnage using the canals continued to increase throughout the nineteenth century. Barges, although horse-drawn, could carry very heavy loads cheaply. Gasworks needed coal supplied directly to the processing plants. As a consequence many gasworks were established along the canals, but with the advent of electrical power and the motorcar in the early twentieth century, the canals went into decline. By 1960, the tonnage moved through London canals had diminished to such an extent that they were no longer commercially viable. The Regent's Canal closed to commercial traffic in 1969.

FROM TOWPATH TO FOOTPATH

Following the Second World War and the decline in canal traffic, the towpaths fell into disrepair through lack of use and poor maintenance. These paths were neither intended nor designed for public access.

Between 1968 and 1982 the towpaths were incrementally repaired and opened to the public. Two factors brought this about; action by the local councils through which the canals ran and the needs of the Central Electricity

Generating Board. The City of Westminster was the first local council to restore the towpath as a thoroughfare for walkers and cyclists. Camden and other councils followed soon after.

The then Central Electricity Generating Board needed to run 400kV cables from its substation in St John's Wood to the East End of London. Normally this would have involved digging up major roads to lay the cables but instead they bought the towpath from Lisson Grove to the Hertford Union Canal, adjacent to Victoria Park. This was a cheaper option; in addition, they could use water from the canal to cool the cables. The flagstones are unfixed for access and can sound like a primitive vibraphone when cycled over.

There are several sections adjacent to the towpaths in this book that are undergoing massive redevelopment, especially in the King's Cross and Queen Elizabeth Olympic Park areas. These landscapes will change as they have done so many times over the past 200 years. These canals and their towpaths will continue to provide a great ways to see parts of London from another perspective.

The route is marked throughout by a red dotted line. Many road and footbridges have steps down to the canals but not in every case. I've marked those where steps exist with a red step symbol.

● ● ● ● Towpath route

● ● ● ● Alternative route

⌐ Stepped access to and from the street

LITTLE VENICE

This is the westernmost point of the Regent's Canal, and the point where it joins the Grand Union Canal in Paddington. The triangular expanse of water, Browning's Pool, is a tranquil place, though not far from the bustle and noise of the elevated A40 Westway, Paddington station and the West End.

1 The Grand Junction Canal

The Grand Junction Canal, built between 1793 and 1805, connected the Midlands with London and the River Thames at Brentford. In 1801, a canal spur, the Paddington Branch, was completed and connected to the recently built New Road (now Marylebone Road and Euston Road). This allowed for goods to be moved by road between the Pool of London in the City and the Paddington Basin. However, large barge loads had to be split up and transferred to horse and wagons. A pressing need existed to extend the canal further east to the River Thames, where it could reach the larger sailing vessels navigating east beyond the Pool of London. By 1810, a plan for a new canal that would connect the Grand Junction to the navigable Thames was being considered.

Grand Junction Canal

Blomfield Road

Waterbus
The London Waterbus Company provides cruises on the Regent's Canal fro...

Robert Browning
1812–89

Following the death of his wife Elizabeth Barratt Browning in 1861, Robert Browning moved back to London, from Italy, and lived in a house (now demolished) on Warwick Crescent until 1887. It is believed that he referred to the area around The Broadwater as 'Little Venice'. The Broadwater was later renamed 'Browning's Pool' in his honour. He died in his son's house in Venice and his body lies in Poets' Corner in Westminster Abbey. The majority of Warwick Crescent is now occupied with a modern, curved block of maisonettes *(above)*.

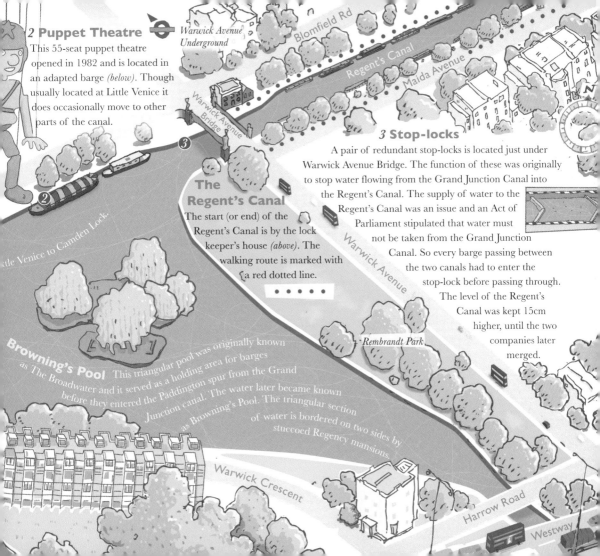

2 Puppet Theatre

This 55-seat puppet theatre opened in 1982 and is located in an adapted barge *(below)*. Though usually located at Little Venice it does occasionally move to other parts of the canal.

Warwick Avenue Underground

The Regent's Canal

The start (or end) of the Regent's Canal is by the lock keeper's house *(above)*. The walking route is marked with a red dotted line.

3 Stop-locks

A pair of redundant stop-locks is located just under Warwick Avenue Bridge. The function of these was originally to stop water flowing from the Grand Junction Canal into the Regent's Canal. The supply of water to the Regent's Canal was an issue and an Act of Parliament stipulated that water must not be taken from the Grand Junction Canal. So every barge passing between the two canals had to enter the stop-lock before passing through. The level of the Regent's Canal was kept 15cm higher, until the two companies later merged.

Rembrandt Park

Browning's Pool This triangular pool was originally known as The Broadwater and it served as a holding area for barges before they entered the Paddington spur from the Grand Junction canal. The water later became known as Browning's Pool. The triangular section of water is bordered on two sides by stuccoed Regency mansions.

Little Venice to Camden Lock

Blomfield Rd

Regent's Canal

Maida Avenue

Warwick Avenue Bridge

Warwick Avenue

Warwick Crescent

Harrow Road

Westway

MAIDA VALE

Warwick Avenue – Maida Hill Tunnel 440m

This genteel, tree-lined length of the Regent's Canal is bordered on both sides by the stuccoed houses, porticoed villas and terraces of Blomfield Road and Maida Avenue. This is the only stretch of the Regent's Canal where the towpath is closed to the public, as the embankments are occupied by privately moored barges and houseboats. However the canal is clearly visible from the adjacent footpaths, which rise up as the canal enters the Maida Hill Tunnel. The canal defines the southern edge of Maida Vale.

1 The Lock Keeper's House

This was built in 1819 at the insistence of the Grand Junction Canal Company, to house the toll collector and to ensure no water flowed into the Regent's Canal.

Warwick Avenue Underground

2 Blomfield Road

The stuccoed buildings of Blomfield Road and Maida Avenue were built between 1830 and 1850, not long after the canal was opened. The new residents were not put off in spite the industrial cargo being shifted only yards away from their front doors.

Blomfield Road

Maida Avenue

Warwick Avenue Bridge

I must go down to the seas again, to the lonely sea and sk And all I ask is a t ship and a star to st her by. SEA FEVE

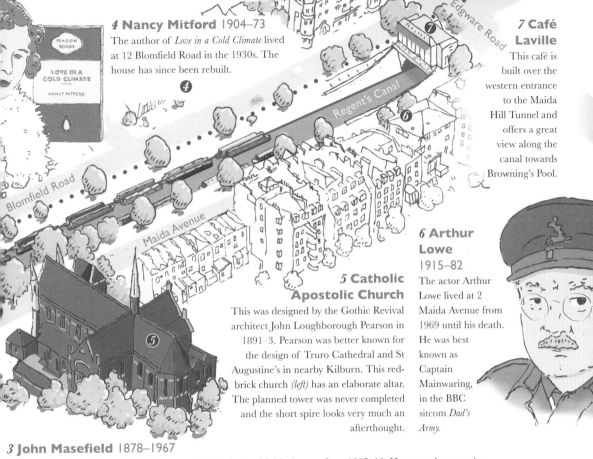

4 Nancy Mitford 1904–73

The author of *Love in a Cold Climate* lived at 12 Blomfield Road in the 1930s. The house has since been rebuilt.

7 Café Laville

This café is built over the western entrance to the Maida Hill Tunnel and offers a great view along the canal towards Browning's Pool.

6 Arthur Lowe 1915–82

The actor Arthur Lowe lived at 2 Maida Avenue from 1969 until his death. He was best known as Captain Mainwaring, in the BBC sitcom *Dad's Army*.

5 Catholic Apostolic Church

This was designed by the Gothic Revival architect John Loughborough Pearson in 1891–3. Pearson was better known for the design of Truro Cathedral and St Augustine's in nearby Kilburn. This redbrick church *(left)* has an elaborate altar. The planned tower was never completed and the short spire looks very much an afterthought.

3 John Masefield 1878–1967

The novelist, playwright and Poet Laureate *(left)* lived at 30 Maida Avenue from 1907–12. He wrote the narrative poem 'The Everlasting Mercy' while living at this location in 1911. Masefield was not a refined Oxbridge-educated writer, but a man who had spent many of his formative years at sea. This poem was written with a very frank use of English language and shocked many on its release. A few years later in 1916 he wrote 'Sea Fever'.

MAIDA TUNNEL

As the canal disappears into Maida Hill, the footpath continues over Edgware Road and along Aberdeen Place. The canal emerges into the slope of St John's Wood. It is bounded on the north side by a high concrete retaining wall. The canal remains within this embankment until it passes Regent's Park. Many of the stuccoed buildings have been replaced over the years with contemporary housing, utilitarian electrical substations and railway bridges.

1 Guy Gibson 1918-44

Wing Commander Guy Gibson was the pilot leader of the Dambusters (bouncing bomb) raid on the Ruhr Valley in May 1943. For this and other bombing raids he received the Victoria Cross. He lived at 32 Aberdeen Place shortly after the Dambuster raid. Later that year he went on a lecture tour of the United States. Gibson returned to active service in 1944 but was killed when the Mosquito he was flying over the Netherlands crash-landed.

Aberdeen Place

2 Crocker's Folly

Formerly called The Crown Hotel, it was built by Frank Crocker and designed by C.H. Worley in 1898 and was believed to be a speculative venture, anticipating the arrival of the Great Central Railway's new London terminus in the vicinity (though the new line had been given Parliamentary approval five years earlier). However, Marylebone Station was built about a kilometre away, adjacent to Marylebone Road. Contrary to certain myths Crocker did not commit suicide within the hotel as a result of bankruptcy, but died in 1904 of natural causes. The hotel and pub, with sumptuous late-Victorian interiors, is now a Grade II listed building. It is now run as Lebanese restaurant and has retained the name Crocker's Folly.

CENTRAL ELECTRICITY
GENERATING BOARD
WARNING
HIGH VOLTAGE CABLES
IN TOWPATH

400kV High Voltage Cables

Adjacent to the metal staircase that descends (46 steps), to the canal from Aberdeen Place, is a large turquoise blue metal conduit that carries high tension electric cables down from a substation to the canal towpath. In 1982 the then Central Electricity Generating Board bought the rights to lay cables from this point to the Hertford Union Canal. The water from the canal is used to cool the high-tension cables. The laying of the cable vastly improved the surface of the towpath for walkers and cyclists. The same year also saw the final stretch of the towpath being opened through to Limehouse.

alternative path

Lisson Gr

Regent's Canal

4 Eyre's Tunnel 48m

Sometimes known as Lisson Grove Tunnel, unlike the Maida Hill Tunnel, this can be walked through. Named after the landowner, Henry Eyre, whose land the canal cut through. The barge horses would be walked from the western entrance of the Maida Hill Tunnel across Edgware Road and Lisson Grove then down to the towpath. They then doubled back westwards along the towpath before joining up with the barges again.

3 Maida Hill Tunnel 250m

This 250m straight tunnel *(left)* was started in 1812. It has no towpath so cannot be walked through. Originally the horses towing the barges would be unhitched and walked over Maida Hill, while the barges were 'legged' through the tunnel. The bargees would lay on planks fixed to the barge and 'walk' along the tunnel walls.

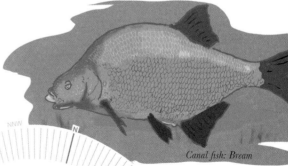

Canal fish: Bream

NNW   N

LISSON GROVE Eyre's Tunnel – Park Road 505m

Once through Eyre's Tunnel the canal opens into a much wider section. This was originally for commercial barges to load and unload at the Great Central Railway goods yard on the southern bank and to supply coal to the Grove Road generating station on the north side. Neither now survives. There are two paths north and south of the canal; the original towpath passes through the private mooring and is only open between certain hours. The alternate path *(shown below)* provides good views of the moored narrowboats.

1 Canal House
120 Lisson Grove

The entrance to this house *(left)* is on the upper storey on Lisson Grove and so is known locally as the 'Upside Down House'. It was built in 1902 for the manager responsible for controlling the barges that supplied coal to the electricity station. The house faces on to the canal and overlooks the moored narrowboats. It is the only house that straddles the Regent's Canal.

2 Grove Road Electrical Substation

Located just above the north bank of the canal is an EDF electricity substation supplying power to the west of London. Originally the plant was a coal-powered electricity station. Coal was brought by barge from the north of England and by sea via the Limehouse Basin. The power generating facility was demolished in 1973 and converted into a substation.

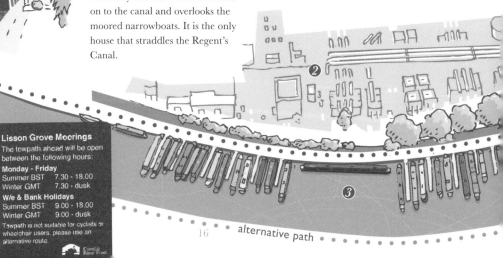

Lisson Grove

Lisson Grove Moorings
The towpath ahead will be open between the following hours:
Monday - Friday
Summer BST   7.30 - 18.00
Winter GMT   7.30 - dusk
W/e & Bank Holidays
Summer BST   9.00 - 18.00
Winter GMT   9.00 - dusk
Towpath is not suitable for cyclists or wheelchair users, please use an alternative route.

Canal & River Trust

alternative path

Lord's Cricket Ground

In 1811 Thomas Lord moved his cricket ground from Dorset Fields (now Dorset Square) off Marylebone Road to a location west of Park Road Bridge (a plaque marks the spot on the south bank). Unfortunately the ground was in the path of the proposed canal. The Regent's Canal Company paid Lord £4,000 (plus the spoils from the Maida Hill Tunnel for the new ground) to move the ground about 500 metres further north-west and save the canal an expensive detour. Lord's Cricket Ground, the home of the Marylebone Cricket Club, moved to its current home *(above)* on St John's Wood Road in 1814.

Right: This brick-built tower is a ventilation shaft for the Jubilee line.

3 Lisson Grove Moorings

This private mooring, opened in 1967, is a small community of about fifty narrowboats. Many have small gardens tucked into the towpath. The Canal is so wide at this point the barges can moor stern on. The towpath is only open during specific hours *(see notice board, left)*. Cycling is not permitted on the mooring towpath.

4 Railway Bridges

The former Great Central Railway line now runs from Aylesbury and Banbury into Marylebone station. The second, eastern bridge carries the Metropolitan Underground line from Baker Street to Amersham and Watford. The whole area to the west of the railway lines was a goods yard that transshipped goods between the canal and rail. It is now largely residential property.

Right: This weathercock, depicting Old Father Time removing a cricket stump, sits on the top of the New Mound Stand at Lord's Cricket Ground.

Regent's Canal

Park Road

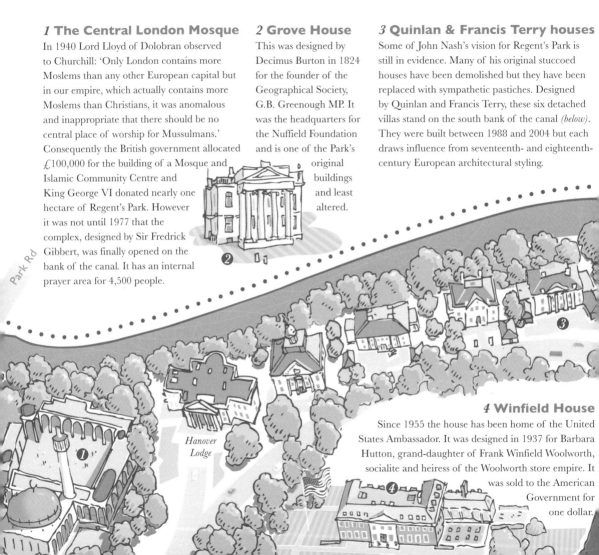

1 The Central London Mosque

In 1940 Lord Lloyd of Dolobran observed to Churchill: 'Only London contains more Moslems than any other European capital but in our empire, which actually contains more Moslems than Christians, it was anomalous and inappropriate that there should be no central place of worship for Mussulmans.' Consequently the British government allocated £100,000 for the building of a Mosque and Islamic Community Centre and King George VI donated nearly one hectare of Regent's Park. However it was not until 1977 that the complex, designed by Sir Fredrick Gibbert, was finally opened on the bank of the canal. It has an internal prayer area for 4,500 people.

Park Rd

2 Grove House

This was designed by Decimus Burton in 1824 for the founder of the Geographical Society, G.B. Greenough MP. It was the headquarters for the Nuffield Foundation and is one of the Park's original buildings and least altered.

3 Quinlan & Francis Terry houses

Some of John Nash's vision for Regent's Park is still in evidence. Many of his original stuccoed houses have been demolished but they have been replaced with sympathetic pastiches. Designed by Quinlan and Francis Terry, these six detached villas stand on the south bank of the canal *(below)*. They were built between 1988 and 2004 but each draws influence from seventeenth- and eighteenth-century European architectural styling.

Hanover Lodge

4 Winfield House

Since 1955 the house has been home of the United States Ambassador. It was designed in 1937 for Barbara Hutton, grand-daughter of Frank Winfield Woolworth, socialite and heiress of the Woolworth store empire. It was sold to the American Government for one dollar.

REGENT'S PARK

Once past the Park Road railway bridges, the landscape becomes very verdant as the canal enters the Regent's Park. It is the least urban of all the sections. The canal was to have originally cut straight across the park, but the new residents, in 1812 did not want the canal, with industrial cargoes, barges and bargees, ruining the vista. So the canal had to arc around the northern perimeter of the Park cutting through the lower sections of St John's Wood Hill. This at least avoided creating several expensive canal locks. The Regent's Canal promoters thought the waterway would enhance the Park.

Prince Albert Road

Chalbert footbridge

Regent's Canal

Macclesfield Bridge

5 River Tyburn

Like most of London's rivers, the Tyburn is buried for most of its length. The two tributaries of the Tyburn start in Hampstead, merge and head south. It crosses over the Regent's Canal in an aqueduct over which the Chalbert footbridge was built. The Tyburn once filled the ornamental lake within the Park. However, pollution brought this to an end. The subterranean stream enters the Thames at Pimlico.

Outer Circle

Decimus Burton 1800–81

The prolific architect and garden designer Decimus Burton *(left)* was responsible for seven of the original buildings in Regent's Park, including Hanover Lodge (1827), Grove House *(opposite page)*, the Clock Tower and the Giraffe House within London Zoo, which he also laid out. He went on to design Hyde Park and the Wellington Arch. But Burton is probably best known for his layout of the Royal Botanic Gardens, Kew and the design of the Palm House and Temperate House there. His body is buried in Kensal Green Cemetery.

I ♥ KEW

The canal arcs around the northern end of # LONDON ZOO

Regent's Park. The towpath is broad and both sides of the embanked canal are lined with trees. There is an additional path that snakes up the northern embankment and connects with Prince Albert Road. The major feature along the second half of this length is London Zoo. The zoo straddles both sides of the canal but the buildings, with the exception of the Snowdon Aviary, appear to shun the canal and all who walk, cycle and sail by. It should be remembered that the zoo was designed at a time when the canal was a foul-smelling industrial highway.

1 Macclesfield Bridge (Blow Up Bridge)

In the early hours of 2 October 1874 a barge, the *Tilbury*, carrying 5 tons of gunpowder and petroleum, exploded while travelling under Macclesfield Bridge. It was reported that a cabin fire ignited the petrol vapour. Three of the crew were killed and several houses destroyed. The keel of the *Tilbury* was found 300m away in a household basement. However the embanked sides of the canal reduced the effects of the explosion. The canal was repaired and back in use within five days – such was its commercial value.

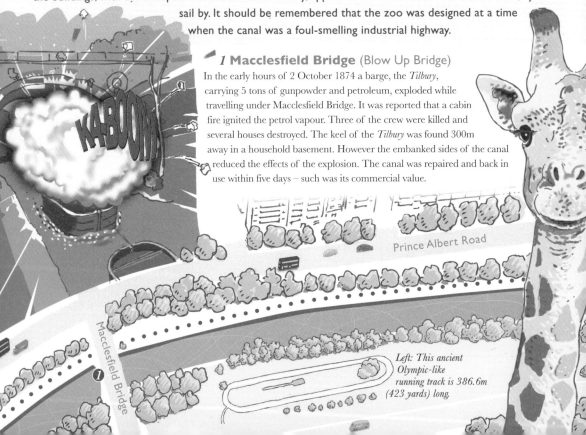

Prince Albert Road

Macclesfield Bridge

Left: This ancient Olympic-like running track is 386.6m (423 yards) long.

N

2 Primrose Hill

Primrose Hill is immediately north of the Snowdon Aviary. For access, cross over Prince Albert Road when adjacent to the Aviary.

Consider a short detour to take in fantastic views of London

3 ZSL London Zoo (Zoological Society London)

Approaching from the west there is not much to indicate that this is a zoo, until you reach the Snowdon Aviary *(left)*. This looms large over the north bank of the canal. A large metal semi transparent 'tent' of fine wire mesh contains the birds. From the towpath you can get a good view of many species of exotic birds including sacred ibis, little egrets, night herons, waldrapp and African grey-headed gulls. The aviary was designed by Antony Armstrong-Jones, 1st Earl of Snowdon, Cedric Price and Frank Newby, and was opened in 1964. On the south bank is a landing stage for visitors choosing to access the zoo by canal from either Camden Lock or Little Venice. The zoo was originally opened in 1828 and was laid out by Decimus Burton. He also designed many of the original buildings within.

fig. 3. The Sacred Ibis

Right: St Mark's Church

Prince Albert Road

Regent's Canal

Zoo footbridge

St Mark's Bridge

right: Zoological Society London HQ

Outer Circle

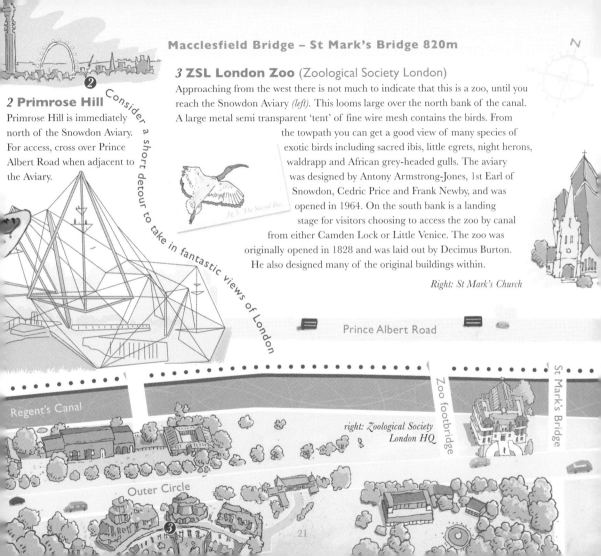

John Nash 1752–1835

One of the most influential people in the development of the Regent's Canal was the architect John Nash. He was born in London and started his career as an architect in 1777. Following a bankruptcy, he moved to Wales and began work there. But by 1795 Nash had moved back to London and was now practising as a successful architect. The most crucial turn in Nash's career came in 1806 when he was appointed 'Surveyor General of Woods, Forests, Parks, and Chases' (manager of the Crown Estates). Effectively he would now be working for the Prince Regent (later King George IV). His first major commission was to create a new thoroughfare, Regent Street, that would link St James's Park with Marylebone Park to the north. Nash was also charged, in 1818, with the redesign of this park, which would become known as Regent's Park. He used the talents of many architects, including James and Decimus Burton (see page 19) to lay out the park with its new gardens, ornamental lakes, ring roads and a zoo. Of the fifty-six stuccoed villas planned, only twenty-six were ever built. Several have since been rebuilt (see page 18). Many of the terrace façades survived (although completely rebuilt internally).

With his royal patronage, Nash had great influence over the design of the expanding London in the early nineteenth century. In 1812,

the Regent's Canal Company was established. Nash became a director and the largest shareholder, having been excited by the prospect of a canal as an urban feature within the park. He originally planned to have the canal run across the park but there was resistance to this idea, so instead it ran as an arc, around the top of the park, cutting through the higher land. This avoided having to create several expensive lock gates and kept the canal out of sight of the new residents.

John Nash went on to design many well known London landmarks, including Marble Arch, All Souls Langham Place (below), Carlton House Terrace, Park Crescent (above) and Buckingham Palace. But when George IV died in 1830, so too did the profligacy on building projects and Nash's career effectively ended. Unlike many of his architectural contemporaries, Nash never received a knighthood. He died five years later at his home on the Isle of Wight. He was criticised for the careless and slipshod nature of many of his buildings but his vision of a new London and especially the Regent's Canal left a remarkable legacy across the capital.

CUMBERLAND SPUR

Once the canal passes St Mark's Bridge it make a sharp left turn under Prince Albert Road, leaving the Regent's Park behind and heading off to into the urban congestion of north London. At this turning there is a short stump that runs south-east from the canal. This is all that now remains of the Cumberland Spur.

1 Feng Shang Princess

Located within the Cumberland Spur, this precarious three-storey 'floating' Chinese restaurant is a very unusual sight on the canal. It's doubtful if it could actually sail.

These railway tracks carry trains from Euston to Birmingham, north-west England and Glasgow (and back).

2 The Cumberland Spur and Market

This canal stump is all that is left of the Cumberland spur. Built in 1830, it ran for 800 metres down to the Cumberland Market, just off Albany Street. The canal barges supplied mainly stone, hay, ice and fresh food products to the Market and the adjacent military barracks. Following the Second World War the Spur fell into decline and it was decommissioned. Rubble from buildings hit during the blitz was used to fill the canal and it is now a car park for Regent's Park. The terracotta stone Gloucester Gate Bridge at the north end of Albany Street passes over what was the canal spur. The canal basin is now, aptly, an allotment for local residents.

Map labels: Regent's Canal · Regent's Park Road · St Mark's Crescent · Gloucester Avenue · Prince Albert Road · Route of the Cumberland Spur · Outer Circle · Regent's Park · Albany Street · Gloucester Gate · Mark's Bridge

23

PIRATE CASTLE

Railway Bridges – Turnover Bridge 275m

The banks of this short stretch of the canal were once home to the producers of Gilbey's Gin. From the 1870s until the 1960s this whole area west of Camden Lock was associated with the wine-importing family, Walter and Alfred Gilbey. The distilleries and warehouses occupied over 8 hectares of land.

1 Pumping Station

On the opposite bank to The Pirate Castle is a pumping station for the National Grid. Built in the same style, it pumps canal water in to cool the high-tension electricity cables under the towpath.

2 The Pirate Castle

This castellated building on the south bank of the canal is home to a water-based club for disadvantaged young people. It was founded in 1966 by Lord St David, designed by Richard Seifert & Partners and was opened in 1977.

3 Academic House

Gilbey's commissioned the modernist architect Serge Chermayeff in 1936 to design a new office block on the corner of Jamestown and Oval Road. Originally named Gilbey House, it is now called Academic House. Chermayeff is best known for the De La Warr Pavilion in Bexhill-on-Sea.

Oval Road

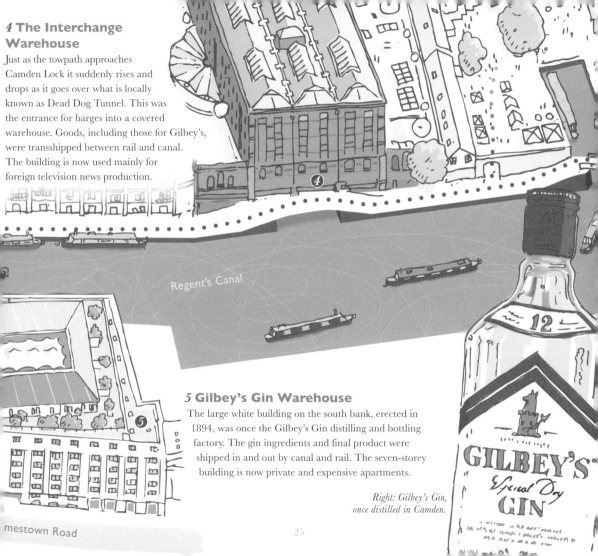

4 The Interchange Warehouse

Just as the towpath approaches Camden Lock it suddenly rises and drops as it goes over what is locally known as Dead Dog Tunnel. This was the entrance for barges into a covered warehouse. Goods, including those for Gilbey's, were transshipped between rail and canal. The building is now used mainly for foreign television news production.

④

Regent's Canal

5 Gilbey's Gin Warehouse

The large white building on the south bank, erected in 1894, was once the Gilbey's Gin distilling and bottling factory. The gin ingredients and final product were shipped in and out by canal and rail. The seven-storey building is now private and expensive apartments.

Right: Gilbey's Gin, once distilled in Camden.

mestown Road

CAMDEN LOCK

Turnover Bridge – Chalk Farm Road Bridge 100m

Camden Lock is without doubt the most visited and busiest area of the all London's canals. Each weekend sees many tens of thousands of tourists flock into the markets, which are one of the most popular attractions in London. Passing through this short section can take some time especially if distracted by all that Camden Lock has to offer. The towpath splits in two as it goes through Camden; one path goes into the Market and Stables, while the second route goes over the Turnover Bridge to the south towpath, over Chalk Farm Road Bridge and rejoins on the north side.

1 **Dingwalls Building** was originally built as stables adjacent to the wharf *(left)* with farrier services for barge towing horses *en route* to Limehouse and the Midlands. These days it is better known as a comedy and music venue. A regular Waterbus service runs from the wharf to Little Venice via the zoo.

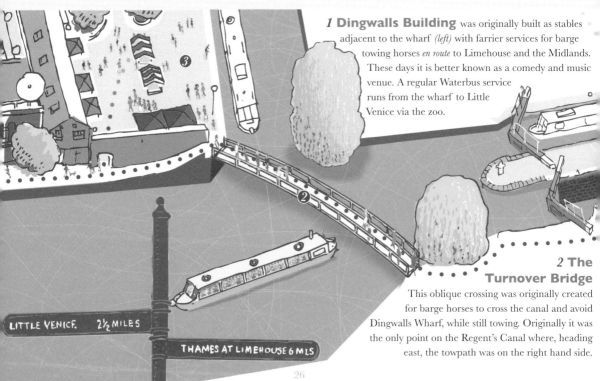

2 **The Turnover Bridge**

This oblique crossing was originally created for barge horses to cross the canal and avoid Dingwalls Wharf, while still towing. Originally it was the only point on the Regent's Canal where, heading east, the towpath was on the right hand side.

LITTLE VENICE. 2½ MILES

THAMES AT LIMEHOUSE 6 MLS

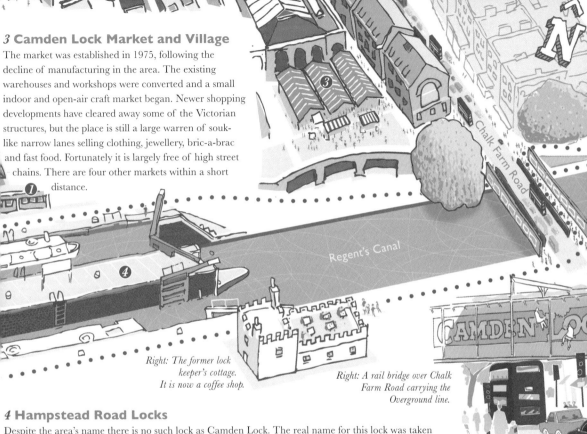

3 Camden Lock Market and Village

The market was established in 1975, following the decline of manufacturing in the area. The existing warehouses and workshops were converted and a small indoor and open-air craft market began. Newer shopping developments have cleared away some of the Victorian structures, but the place is still a large warren of souk-like narrow lanes selling clothing, jewellery, bric-a-brac and fast food. Fortunately it is largely free of high street chains. There are four other markets within a short distance.

Right: The former lock keeper's cottage. It is now a coffee shop.

Right: A rail bridge over Chalk Farm Road carrying the Overground line.

Camden Town Underground

4 Hampstead Road Locks

Despite the area's name there is no such lock as Camden Lock. The real name for this lock was taken from the nearby road, though this is now called Chalk Farm Road. Cruising eastwards, these are the first locks that a barge would encounter for 30km. They are also the only working double pair of locks remaining on the Regent's Canal. Each time the locks are raised or lowered, over 250 cubic metres of water has to be replaced. Initially this was a major problem for the Regent's Canal Company until they created a feeder reservoir, Welsh Harp, in north London close to what is now the North Circular Road.

1 Camden Lock Village

Camden Lock Village, east of Chalk Farm Road, was partially destroyed by fire in 2008, is now being entirely rebuilt. The old market and food stalls are to be replaced by a contemporary structure that is very far removed from the Victorian red brick stables across the road.

4 The Overground

This railway line skirts close to the Regent's Canal at Hawley Lock. The line from Richmond to Stratford carries both passengers and freight. The line was built in the latter half of the nineteenth century after several attempts were made to buy the Regent's Canal with a plan to convert it into a railway. Fortunately these designs never took off. The closest station is about 150m away on Camden Road.

3 Hawley and Kentish Town Locks

These two double locks *(above)*, like all the remaining locks down to Limehouse, have been converted into single locks to save on maintenance. The second lock is now a weir.

5 Elephant House

This two-storey terracotta structure, adjacent to Kentish Town Road Bridge was built in 1900 as a brewery for the production of Elephant Pale Ale. A splendidly carved elephant's head still resides over the main portal on Kentish Town Road.

2 Viacom/MTV studios

Located on the south bank of the canal, this building was formerly the TV-am studios, home of the first national breakfast television programme in the UK. The large gable-end eggcups are still visible from the canal towpath. The frontage and studios on Hawley Street were originally designed by Terry Farrell as an addition to what was once a motor garage. Following its closure it became the European HQ for MTV and Viacom. A living green wall now covers the street facade.

Chalk Farm Road

Kentish Town Road

Regent's Canal

Grand Union Walk

Camden Town Underground

CAMDEN TOWN

Heading east from Camden Lock the towpath becomes less populated. It is no longer the domain of the tourist, but only the occasional walker, cyclist and jogger. The canal zigzags for the next 600m. The planners had to get the canal under six existing roads that radiated out from Camden and create six new bridges over the canal. The least expensive way was to pass under each of them at 90° to the road, rather than cutting them at oblique angles. The canal reaches its northernmost point before heading south-east to Limehouse.

6 Grand Union Walk Housing

This 'futuristic' row of housing pods that overlook the canal were designed by Grimshaw Architects in 1988. Sadly they don't look as sleek and shiny now as when they were first built.

7 River Fleet

The River Fleet is a major tributary of the Thames. But for the past 150 years for most of its journey it has snaked underground from its sources in Hampstead. In the 1600s, when it was an open river, it was reported to be 8m wide in Camden. It crosses beneath the canal at a point near Camden Road and Lyme Street. It is buried 5m below ground.

8 Joe Slovo & Ruth First

Joe Slovo, a leading member of the African National Congress and the South African Communist Party, lived in exile with his wife Ruth First at 13 Lyme Street from 1966 until 1978.

29

The Battle for the Canal

In 1810, the barrister William Agar purchased 29 hectares of land south-east of Camden, having possibly been tipped off that the canal would cross this land. Two years later he opposed the Regent's Canal Act and the route the canal would take through his estate. Even after the Regent's Canal Company had compensated him, he still resisted the construction of the canal.

In 1815 Agar had his estate staff attempt to prevent the canal construction workers access to his land. But the company's navvies used force to enter the estate and start the cutting. The following day a second attempt was made to gain access. This time a Bow Street police officer police was called and two of the canal managers were arrested. The matter was resolved in court with more compensation being paid to Agar. The dispute was a huge financial drain on the Regent's Canal Company and this section of the canal was not completed until 1819. Agar was compensated a total of £15,750. He continued to impede the development of the canal until as late as 1832. Most of the landowners along the length of the canal were commemorated with a bridge or a lock being named after them. This was not the case for Agar.

REGENT'S CANAL? — NOT ON MY ESTATE!

St Pancras Way

Regent's Canal

Royal College St

St Pancras

The Waterfront

Hardly any of the original structures built close to the canal were designed to overlook it (the housing in Maida Vale and Regent's Park were set well back from the canal). Barges carrying many types of cargo, including chemicals, dynamite and horse manure were not considered picturesque or desirable (or safe, following the barge explosion in Regent's Park in 1874). However, once the canal traffic ceased in the 1960s and local councils opened the former towpaths to the public twenty years later, property developers saw the attractions of buying up relatively cheap disused warehousing and factories, and demolishing them or converting them into living spaces, with balconies overlooking the canal. The canal-side house building still continues apace.

ELM VILLAGE

The canal, having wriggled its way through Camden, now enters a long, bleak, straight section heading south-east towards St Pancras. The canal banks are lined with mainly housing, warehouses and offices. The vista is only relieved by new flats and apartments that have appeared in the past few years.

Agar Town

A low-quality housing development was built, in 1841, on the south-eastern edge of the Agar estate, adjacent to the canal and the rubbish mounds. Known as Agar Town, it quickly became a slum area and was referred to by Dickens in *Household Words* in 1851. Within twenty-five years it was demolished to make way for the St Pancras station marshalling yards. However, in the 1970s the railway tracks were removed and a new housing estate, Elm Village was built on the land in 1983.

Canal fish: Carp

▷ *To Paris, Brussels and the Midlands*

Camley Street

1 The Ugly Brown Building

The fashion retailer Ted Baker has a large, squat anonymous warehouse (formerly a Royal Mail sorting office) adjacent to the canal. It irreverently addresses itself as The Ugly Brown Building, 6a St Pancras Way.

ST PANCRAS

Camley Street Bridge – canal bend 405m

The towpath, once beyond Camley Street Bridge, enters an area that is undergoing a massive redevelopment. The two sets of railway lines of St Pancras and King's Cross stations and the land in between have already undergone huge changes in the past seventeen years. St Pancras is now the terminus for Eurostar. Sleek white trains roar away to France and Belgium while sedate narrowboats chug slowly along the canal below. Sandwiched between these two ages of transport is a nature park. Further development is underway turning 27 hectares of old railway land into residential, education, shopping and business developments.

A Eurostar train

Camley Street

1 Coal Drops Yard

The Great Northern Railway built this depot with a basin and covered transshipment facilities. Barges could access the basin via a tunnel immediately south of St Pancras Lock. Part of this building is being redeveloped into retail and restaurant facilities. The original gas holder structures have been converted into three sets of circular flats. These Grade II listed gas holders sat south of the nearby Camley Street Natural Park and once featured in the 1965 film *Alfie*.

2 St Pancras Cruising Club

This inlet, originally named St Pancras Basin, was a rail terminal. It was created in 1846, before any other railways in the area, to bring coal from Doncaster to the adjacent gasworks. But after the gasworks demise in 1945 it became home to the St Pancras Cruising Club. Originally the club catered for wood and fibre glass built boats, though it is now predominately occupied by narrowboats. The development of St Pancras International immediately to the west has threatened the existence of the club several times.

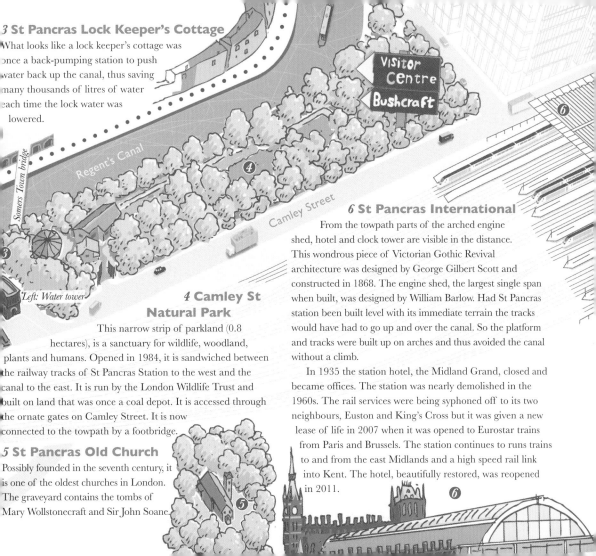

3 St Pancras Lock Keeper's Cottage

What looks like a lock keeper's cottage was once a back-pumping station to push water back up the canal, thus saving many thousands of litres of water each time the lock water was lowered.

Left: Water tower

4 Camley St Natural Park

This narrow strip of parkland (0.8 hectares), is a sanctuary for wildlife, woodland, plants and humans. Opened in 1984, it is sandwiched between the railway tracks of St Pancras Station to the west and the canal to the east. It is run by the London Wildlife Trust and built on land that was once a coal depot. It is accessed through the ornate gates on Camley Street. It is now connected to the towpath by a footbridge.

5 St Pancras Old Church

Possibly founded in the seventh century, it is one of the oldest churches in London. The graveyard contains the tombs of Mary Wollstonecraft and Sir John Soane.

6 St Pancras International

From the towpath parts of the arched engine shed, hotel and clock tower are visible in the distance. This wondrous piece of Victorian Gothic Revival architecture was designed by George Gilbert Scott and constructed in 1868. The engine shed, the largest single span when built, was designed by William Barlow. Had St Pancras station been built level with its immediate terrain the tracks would have had to go up and over the canal. So the platform and tracks were built up on arches and thus avoided the canal without a climb.

In 1935 the station hotel, the Midland Grand, closed and became offices. The station was nearly demolished in the 1960s. The rail services were being syphoned off to its two neighbours, Euston and King's Cross but it was given a new lease of life in 2007 when it was opened to Eurostar trains from Paris and Brussels. The station continues to runs trains to and from the east Midlands and a high speed rail link into Kent. The hotel, beautifully restored, was reopened in 2011.

KING'S CROSS

The Regent's Canal arrived over thirty years before the two adjacent stations. These two modes of transport managed to co-exist for some period of time and mutually benefited from each other, but ultimately the railways would send the canal traffic into decline. The canal and towpath are now an area of calm in this deluge of redevelopment at King's Cross. There are currently some fantastic urban views of King's Cross and St Pancras railway stations from the towpath and the new bridge, though these are slowly becoming obscured by the new office buildings to the south of the canal.

Left: The Coal Office

Stop-locks

Camley Street Natural Park

Regent's Canal

Imperial Gas Light and Coke Company

Not long after the canal was opened, a gasworks was established on this side of the canal. Gas for lighting the houses and streets of London was extracted from coal. The canals made the transportation of this raw, heavy material much more efficient than horse and wagons. The gas holders, now listed, have been restored and have been rebuilt as apartments on the northern bank *(see previous page)*.

1 King's Cross station

The railway terminus was designed by the engineer George Turnbull and Lewis Cubitt and built in 1852. The rail tracks running out of King's Cross tunnelled under the canal, because early steam locomotives had a problem hauling carriages up the slope from a standing start (St Pancras engineers would chose to elevate the

34

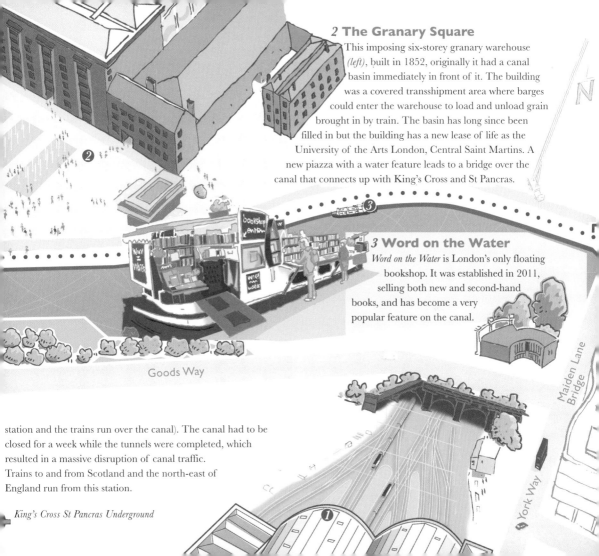

2 The Granary Square

This imposing six-storey granary warehouse *(left)*, built in 1852, originally it had a canal basin immediately in front of it. The building was a covered transshipment area where barges could enter the warehouse to load and unload grain brought in by train. The basin has long since been filled in but the building has a new lease of life as the University of the Arts London, Central Saint Martins. A new piazza with a water feature leads to a bridge over the canal that connects up with King's Cross and St Pancras.

3 Word on the Water

Word on the Water is London's only floating bookshop. It was established in 2011, selling both new and second-hand books, and has become a very popular feature on the canal.

Goods Way

Maiden Lane Bridge

station and the trains run over the canal). The canal had to be closed for a week while the tunnels were completed, which resulted in a massive disruption of canal traffic. Trains to and from Scotland and the north-east of England run from this station.

King's Cross St Pancras Underground

York Way

1 Stop-locks

The railway lines in and out of King's Cross station go under the Regent's Canal. During the Second World War, Luftwaffe bombers targeted this section of the canal. Had the canal been breeched here the railway line would have been flooded and traffic to and from the north severely disrupted. Stop-locks were fitted to the canal on either side of the railway line. Once the air raid siren sounded the stop-locks were closed. The eastern set can still be seen embedded within the canal bank immediately after the Maiden Lane Bridge.

3 Battlebridge Basin

Prior to 1830 the area now known as King's Cross was referred to as Battlebridge. The 'bridge' was a few hundred metres to the west and crossed the now culverted River Fleet. The basin was opened in 1825 and comprised of a beer bottling plant, a timber yard plus warehousing for corn, salt, and imported fruit. J. Dickenson had a paper warehouse located at the southern end of the basin. While some of the original wharfs remain, many have been converted or demolished to make way for waterside offices and apartments. The basin is now used for private moorings.

Maiden Lane Bridge

York Way

King's Cross St Pancras Underground

KINGS CROSS

2 Kings Place

Kings Place is built on what was once the Great Northern Distillery Wharf. The centre opened in 2008 as a venue for classical and jazz concerts, contemporary arts and spoken events. It is also home to the *Guardian* and *Observer* media offices.

4 London Canal Museum

The museum was opened in 1992 as a home to a collection of canal artefacts, memorabilia and displays portraying the history of canal growth and decline in Britain. There is a reconstructed cabin showing the cramped conditions experienced by canal workers and their families.

CORO

New Wharf Road

The Guardian

Wharfdale Road

BATTLEBRIDGE BASIN

York Way (Maiden Lane Bridge) – West Tunnel entrance 520m

Once through Maiden Lane Bridge, the construction works are left behind and the environment around the towpath becomes much quieter again. Immediately to the right is the Battlebridge Basin and the Kings Place. This is a straight section that clings to the contour line. The canal engineers decided to enable quicker transport times by avoiding building a series of locks up and over Islington Hill and tunnelling through to the City Basin instead. Sadly, the only way to view the inside of the tunnel is by water; walkers and cyclists have to travel over the hill.

Right: A detail of the cut-out stencilled work on Thornhill Bridge

Thornhill Wharf

Thornhill Bridge

Caledonian Road

Regent's Canal

Muriel Street

Wynford Road

5 Gatti's Ice House

In 1856, the Swiss-born Carlo Gatti started importing ice into London. Earlier he had been cutting ice, under contract, from the Regent's Canal! By 1863 he had built a storage unit that is now the London Canal Museum. Huge blocks of ice were cut from Norwegian fjords and shipped to the Limehouse Canal Basin and there transferred to barges and on to the storage unit in Battlebridge. The ice was stored in two wells 10m wide by 13m deep, before being transported around London.

ISLINGTON TUNNEL

West Tunnel entrance – Danbury Street Bridge 1,330m (including connecting walk)

The tunnel is nearly 900m in length and, like Maida Hill Tunnel, has no towpath. The barge horses had to be unharnessed and walked over the hill. At the eastern end of the Tunnel there are towpaths on either side of the canal – quite rare for the Regent's Canal. However, be warned the southern towpath takes you into the City Basin and away from the main route to Limehouse.

Over the hill

There are numerous ways to cross over Islington Hill on foot or by cycle. Once off the canal, turn right into Muriel Street, crossing over the tunnel mouth, then turn left into Wynford Street. Follow the pedestrian path to Panton Street. Turn right, cross the road and continue into Chapel Market. This is a daily street market (open every day except Monday). Turn right into Liverpool Street, left into busy Upper Street. Cut across Upper Street and the antique shop festooned Camden Passage. The York public house marks the corner of Duncan Street. Continue down Duncan Street and at the end is a set of iron railings and a drop down to the Regent's Canal.

This route takes in

Muriel Street

Wynford Road

Panton Street

Liverpool Street

Chapel Market, a daily street market (open every day except Monday), across the busy **Upper Street**

Chapel Market

1 Islington Tunnel

The Tunnel was built to avoid having to create a series of locks up and over Islington Hill. Re-routing the canal to the south was impossible as the area was already built up. The tunnel was completed in 1818, though didn't open until 1820 due to cashflow problems. The tunnel consists of 4 million bricks and is 886m long. The horses towing the barges had to be led over Islington Hill while the barges were 'legged' through the tunnel. This was slow and hard work. In the 1820s several powered solutions were tested, including a moving chain and several steam powered tugs. Signalmen were employed at each end of the tunnel to control the traffic. This system continued to be used for eighty years until the introduction of a diesel tug made the chain haulage system redundant.

2 The Business Design Centre

This was formerly known as the Royal Agricultural Hall, but despite its name it was an exhibition centre for a great variety of non-agrarian shows and events during the nineteenth and early twentieth centuries. After a major refurbishment it was reincarnated as the Business Design Centre and was reopened in 1986.

3 Camden Passage

This pedestrianised thoroughfare is renowned for its variety of antiques shops. It was founded in the 1960s but following the regeneration of the area in the 1980s, rent increases are beginning to force many of the shop owners out. There is an antiques market every Wednesday, Friday, Saturday and Sunday.

4 Joe Orton 1933–1967

The playwright Joe Orton lived his final years in a bedsit flat at 25 Noel Road, Islington. Orton authored several black farces during his short career, including *Loot*, *Entertaining Mr Sloane* and *What the Butler Saw*. It was at this address that he was bludgeoned to death by his lover, Kenneth Halliwell, in August 1967. Halliwell committed suicide immediately afterwards. Just before his death Orton had been writing a film script, *Up Against It*, for the Beatles. It was never filmed.

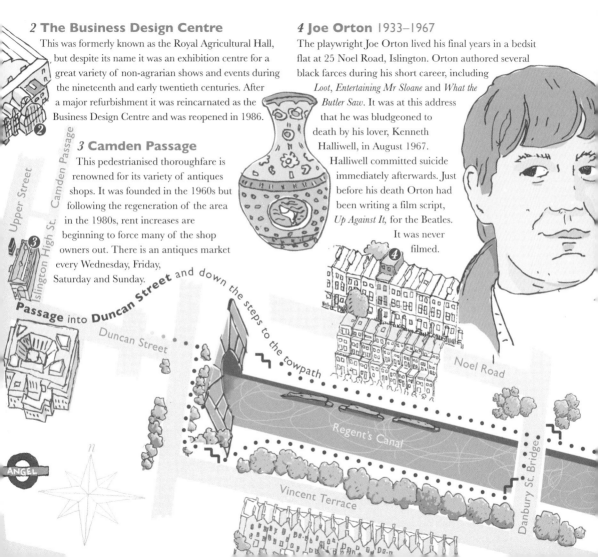

Upper Street

Islington High St.

Camden Passage

Passage into **Duncan Street** and down the steps to the towpath

Duncan Street

Noel Road

ANGEL

Regent's Canal

Vincent Terrace

Danbury St. Bridge

CITY ROAD BASIN

Danbury Street Bridge – New North Road Bridge 845m

The City Road Locks mark the halfway point of the Regent's Canal. Here the vista opens out to the south into the City Road Basin. Once past the basin the canal heads straight, in a north-easterly direction, towards Haggerston. Both sides of the canal are occupied by elderly factories and offices that are slowly giving way to new residences overlooking the waterway.

Angel Underground

1 City Road Basin

The basin was built to serve the city of London, located less than a mile away to the south-east of the basin. It is now 1.6 hectares in size. Opened in 1819, it was surrounded by wharfs for flour, timber and later pharmaceuticals. Coal was also off loaded for the nearby gasworks. The removal company Pickfords had a large wharf and headquarters on a section of the basin that extended south, under the City Road. This area was filled in during the 1930s. The name Pickford Wharf still survives, though it is now residential housing that occupies the site. The basin is now used by the Islington Boat Club which formed in 1970.

The Islington Boat Club

City Road Locks

below: The Narrowboat pub

2 Wenlock Basin

This basin opened in 1826 as the City Road Basin became full to capacity. It was partially filled on the western side for commercial buildings in 1967. The northern end is used mainly for private mooring these days. While the southern end has silted up and become a haven for wildlife.

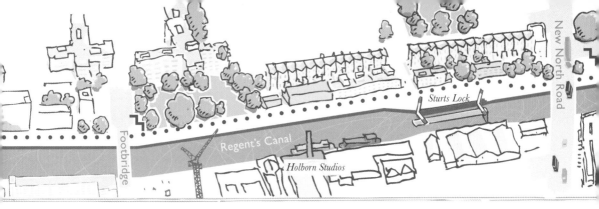

Sturts Lock

New North Road

Regent's Canal

Footbridge

Holborn Studios

Thomas Homer

The main protagonist of the Regent's Canal was Thomas Homer. He owned several barges on the Grand Junction Canal. Shortly after the opening of the Paddington branch of the Grand Junction Canal in 1802, Homer first schemed a plan to link The Broadwater at Little Venice and the River Thames at Limehouse, adjacent to the Limehouse Cut. It was not until 1810 that Homer was able to revive his plan when he heard of John Nash's plans for the proposed Regent's Park. The two men met and Homer presented his idea for the 'London Canal', as it was then known. Nash was very enthusiastic and saw how it could be accommodated within his grand schemes.

It was calculated that the 13.5km canal would cost £280,000. The plans were formulated and a bill was presented to Parliament. It was Nash who would use his influence and royal patronage to drive the project through. Once Royal assent was granted in 1812, the Regent's Canal Company lost little time in starting the project. A working committee was formed with Homer appointed as superintendent of the canal works. Owing to an earlier bankruptcy

he never became a shareholder.

By 1815 the Company was facing financial problems on several fronts: the Agar Estate (see page 30), overrunning costs and doubts about the accounting methods used by Homer. Realising that his acts of embezzlement of company funds had been uncovered, he fled the country. A 100 guinea reward was offered for Homer's successful arrest. Homer headed first to Belgium and then to Scotland. The Company learning of his movements sent an agent to arrest Homer. He was tried, found guilty, sentenced and transported to Australia for seven years. The man who schemed and planned the Regent's Canal was never formally recognised as its innovator. No lock or bridge was ever named after him.

1 Alfred Hitchcock 1899–1980

One of the UK's greatest film directors, Alfred Hitchcock, began work as a title designer at what was to become the Gainsborough Film Studios located just off the canal by New North Road in 1920. He was born in nearby Leytonstone and trained as a draughtsman and designer. Within five years he had become a director. He produced many of his successful early psychological thrillers here, including *The 39 Steps* and *The Lady Vanishes*, plus the first UK talkie, *Blackmail*. Hitchcock emigrated to Hollywood in 1939 and continued his successful career. The Gainsborough Studios produced many popular films, including *Oh, Mr Porter!* and *Waterloo Road*. In 1941 the studio facilities were moved to Lime Grove in west London due to the risk of German bombing. The studios were closed in 1951 and eventually converted into a carpet warehouse before being demolished and residential apartments built on the site *(below)*. The new street names reflect the area's brief former glory: Gaumont Terrace and Gainsborough Studios.

2 Stalin in London

The 5th Congress of the Russian Social Democratic Labour Party met at the Brotherhood Church in May 1907, on the corner of Southgate Road and Balmes Road. The Congress, exiled from Tzarist Russia, was attended by several hundred members, including Lenin, Stalin and Trotsky. The church has been demolished and a residential block stands on the site.

Right: A sculpture of Alfred Hitchcock by Antony Donaldson is situated within the courtyard of the Gainsborough Studios (left)

Balmes Road

Southgate Road

New North Road

DE BEAUVOIR

On this length of the canal there is a mixture of twentieth-century social housing, old Victorian factories and warehouses, plus new waterfront developments, especially on the Hoxton side (south). In the early part of the last century, in this unassuming and run-down part of north London, two men would nurture their future careers here. One would become a master of cinematic suspense while the other would go on to become leader of the Soviet empire.

Towpath Cafe
Lunch
Grilled cheese sandwich
Smoked salmon w. fennel salad
Caerphilly cheese + oatcakes
Mushrooms on toast

Toasted Montgomery cheddar sandwich

3 Canalside restaurants and cafés

Over the past few years this short stretch of towpath has seen a remarkably large number of cafés and restaurants appear offering a wide range of food and drink. And over a weekend they can be especially busy with canal walkers, cyclists and families alike. One cafe has even installed a floating pontoon to create extra seating area.

Whitmore Road

Regent's Canal

Kingsland Road

4 Kingsland Basin

The Kingsland Basin is run by 'Canals in Hackney Users Group' (CHUG). It is a self-managed community of boat owners who own the lease of the basin. They are responsible for maintaining the basin, liaising with local communities and organising guided tours of the canal. One of the narrowboats has been converted into a vegetable garden complete with a duck coop. There is also a small kayak slalom course by the entrance to the basin.

Right: Skyline signage above the Gainsborough Studios

GAINSBOROUGH

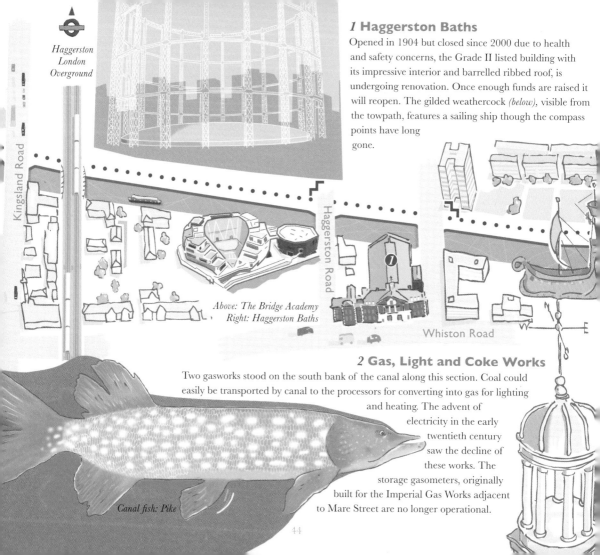

Kingsland Road

1 Haggerston Baths

Opened in 1904 but closed since 2000 due to health and safety concerns, the Grade II listed building with its impressive interior and barrelled ribbed roof, is undergoing renovation. Once enough funds are raised it will reopen. The gilded weathercock *(below)*, visible from the towpath, features a sailing ship though the compass points have long gone.

Haggerston Road

Above: The Bridge Academy
Right: Haggerston Baths

Whiston Road

2 Gas, Light and Coke Works

Two gasworks stood on the south bank of the canal along this section. Coal could easily be transported by canal to the processors for converting into gas for lighting and heating. The advent of electricity in the early twentieth century saw the decline of these works. The storage gasometers, originally built for the Imperial Gas Works adjacent to Mare Street are no longer operational.

Canal fish: Pike

HAGGERSTON

The canal marks the boundary between Hackney to the north and Bethnal Green to the south. The area immediately around the canal is known as Haggerston and was once a hamlet in the Forest of Middlesex. In the nineteenth century, after the arrival of the canal, the fields and farmland were built over with housing for the rapidly expanding London population. Most of the early development has been replaced with various modern adaptations.

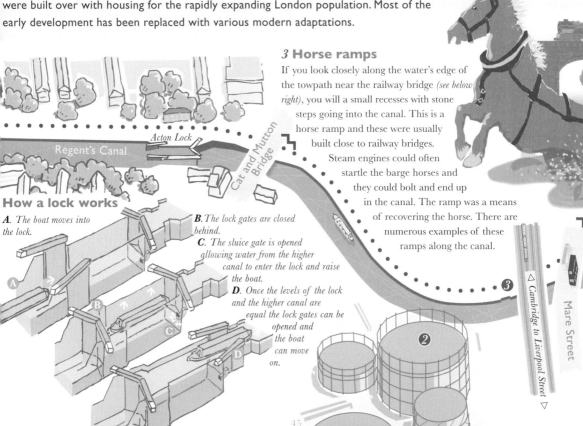

3 Horse ramps

If you look closely along the water's edge of the towpath near the railway bridge *(see below right)*, you will a small recesses with stone steps going into the canal. This is a horse ramp and these were usually built close to railway bridges. Steam engines could often startle the barge horses and they could bolt and end up in the canal. The ramp was a means of recovering the horse. There are numerous examples of these ramps along the canal.

Acton Lock

Regent's Canal

Cat and Mutton Bridge

How a lock works

A. The boat moves into the lock.

B. The lock gates are closed behind.

C. The sluice gate is opened allowing water from the higher canal to enter the lock and raise the boat.

D. Once the levels of the lock and the higher canal are equal the lock gates can be opened and the boat can move on.

△ Cambridge to Liverpool Street ▽

Mare Street

VICTORIA PARK

The urban landscape is transformed once beyond Mare Street. The looming gasometers and factories make way for a more lush and verdant area. As the canal arcs to the right the trees on the left mark the beginnings of Victoria Park. It was built in the 1840s for the residents of the East End as a recreational space, away from the urban sprawl that was engulfing greenfield sites in Hackney and Tower Hamlets. Today it is still a much loved and used open space.

1 Victoria Park

The park was laid out by the second cousin to John Nash, Sir James Pennethorpe (1801–71) between 1842 and 1845. It is still the largest London municipal park. The western part of the park was built on land that had belonged to heretic-burning Bishop Bonner during the reign of Henry VIII. An ornate pedestrian bridge that crosses the canal is named after his residence, Bonner Hall. The bridge and the gates form the main entrance to the park. Just beyond the gates are two statues of dogs on plinths. These are the Dogs of Alcibiades – with docked tails. During the Second World War the park was closed so that anti-aircraft guns could be installed to target German bombers as they attacked the docks and industrial areas of London's East End. However, they too became targets for the bombers and several artefacts in the park were destroyed, including an arcaded shelter designed by Pennethorne. The park has always been used for large political and religious meetings and rallies. The first Rock Against Racism concert was held in the park in 1978. It is still a major music venue during the summer months.

A new Chinese pagoda has been reconstructed on an island within the lake with two connecting bridges. This is part of a £12 million refurbishment project for the park.

2 One of the The Dogs of Alcibiades, guarding the entrance to Victoria Park at Bonner Bridge

Mare Street

Regent's Canal

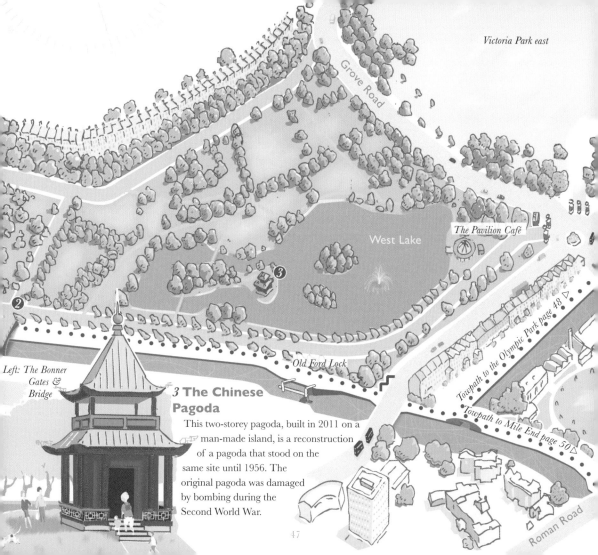

Victoria Park east

Grove Road

West Lake

The Pavilion Café

③

②

Left: The Bonner Gates & Bridge

Old Ford Lock

Towpath to the Olympic Park page 48 ▽

Towpath to Mile End page 50 ▽

3 The Chinese Pagoda

This two-storey pagoda, built in 2011 on a man-made island, is a reconstruction of a pagoda that stood on the same site until 1956. The original pagoda was damaged by bombing during the Second World War.

Roman Road

1 Lakeview Estate

The eleven-storey tower was designed by the modernist architect, Berthold Lubetkin (1901–90). He is best known for the penguin pool in London Zoo and Highpoint, Highgate. It is one of three that he designed in Bethnal Green (now Tower Hamlets) and is an example of the architect's use of precast concrete and love of complex geometric patterns.

2 The Burdett-Coutts drinking fountain

This grandiose gothic drinking fountain, constructed of pink marble and granite, was donated in 1862 by the philanthropist Baroness Angela Burdett-Coutts to provide the people of the East End with clean drinking water.

Victoria Park Road

Victoria Park west

Grove Road

East Lake

Gunmakers Gate

Old Ford Road

Hertford Union Canal

Three Colt Br.

Top Lock

3 Hertford Union Canal

Sir George Duckett, owner of the Stort Navigation (an offshoot of the River Lee Navigation), envisaged the advantages of linking up the River Lee Navigation to the Regent's Canal with a straight 2km interconnecting canal. It would remove a long trip along the Lee, Bow Creek and the Thames to reach the Regent's Canal Dock (at this time the Regent's Canal Dock and Limehouse Cut were not directly linked). The Hertford Union Canal opened in 1831. The initial toll charges were high and the canal usage was fairly minimal. Duckett went bankrupt within a year. In 1855 the Regent's Canal Company bought the canal and took over the running of it.

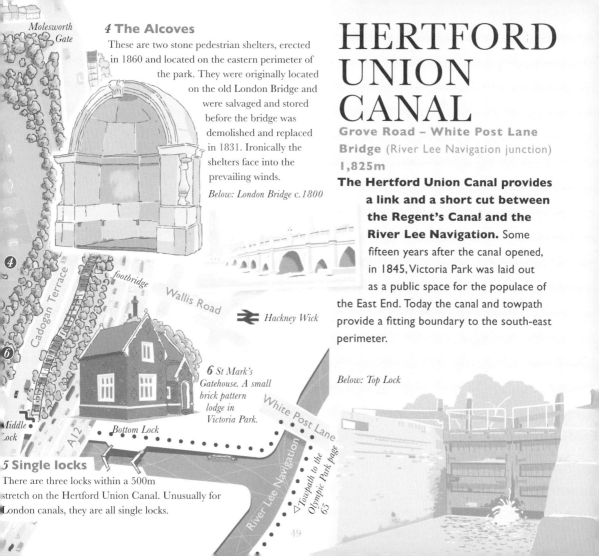

4 The Alcoves

These are two stone pedestrian shelters, erected in 1860 and located on the eastern perimeter of the park. They were originally located on the old London Bridge and were salvaged and stored before the bridge was demolished and replaced in 1831. Ironically the shelters face into the prevailing winds.

Below: London Bridge c.1800

Molesworth Gate

footbridge

Wallis Road

Cadogan Terrace

⇄ *Hackney Wick*

6 St Mark's Gatehouse. A small brick pattern lodge in Victoria Park.

Bottom Lock

Middle Lock

A12

5 Single locks

There are three locks within a 500m stretch on the Hertford Union Canal. Unusually for London canals, they are all single locks.

White Post Lane

River Lee Navigation

△ *Towpath to the Olympic Park page 65*

HERTFORD UNION CANAL

Grove Road – White Post Lane Bridge (River Lee Navigation junction) **1,825m**

The Hertford Union Canal provides a link and a short cut between the Regent's Canal and the River Lee Navigation. Some fifteen years after the canal opened, in 1845, Victoria Park was laid out as a public space for the populace of the East End. Today the canal and towpath provide a fitting boundary to the south-east perimeter.

Below: Top Lock

MILE END

Grove Road

Almost the entire section of the Mile End adjacent to the canal has been transformed over the past twenty years and very little remains of the old industrial East End. The eastern bank is now entirely dominated by the Mile End Park with the Green Bridge. The park is built upon bomb sites from the Second World War. The western bank is dominated by Queen Mary University of London campus plus a variety of new and old residential housing. It is also the location of one of the oldest Jewish cemeteries in the UK.

2 V-1 Flying Bomb

The first Nazi V-1 flying bomb (sometimes referred to as the Doodlebug) fell on the rail bridge at Grove Road on 13 June 1944. Eight civilians were killed in the attack.

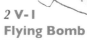

Roman Road

Meath footbridge

1 The Ecology Park

The Ecology Park *(above)* is a collection of lakes, a wind turbine and an energy efficient 'earth sheltered building' that utilises solar power on the large glazed areas. The surrounding parkland is home to rare orchids, moths and spiders. The Palm Tree pub stands alone within the Ecology Park (the Luftwaffe missed it). This early twentieth-century, Grade II hostelry is now closed for redevelopment.

Right: Two gravestones from the Sephardi Novo Beth Chaim cemetery

4 The New Globe Tavern

The pub is all that remains of the much larger pleasure gardens that surrounded it. Opened in 1820, the owner provided many forms of entertainment including ballet and fireworks to attract custom.

Mile End Underground

3 The Arts Pavilion

The Arts Pavilion *(left)* is a community arts gallery that is buried within a man made grassy bank of the Mile End Park. Its large western facing windows overlook ponds and an 'arts mound'. The gallery has a sense of airiness and space.

5 The Green Bridge

Known locally as the 'banana bridge', because of its yellow underside *(above)*. The bridge is covered in grass and sapling trees and forms a 25m pedestrian and cycleway over the busy Mile End Road and links two sections of the Mile End Park. It was designed by Piers Gough of CZWG Architects and opened in 2000.

Mile End Lock

Regent's Canal

6 Sephardi Novo Beth Chaim Cemetery

This is one of the oldest Jewish cemeteries in the UK. Opened in 1725 to replace the Old Sephardi cemetery* and closed in the 1920s. It was the burial place of the Spanish and Portuguese Jews who lived in the area. Originally over 9,000 bodies were laid to rest in this cemetery. Much of the site was deconsecrated in 1973 to make way for the expansion of Queen Mary College. For access, leave the canal at Mile End Bridge and head west across the bridge and turn into Westfield Way. Pass by the building on the left hand side and there, set back is a low wall, is the eastern boundary of what is left of the Sephardi Novo Beth Chaim cemetery.

Westfield Way

* *The oldest surviving UK cemetery, Old Velho Sephardi (1657), is located about 400m away to the west, but is walled and is only accessible by appointment.*

1 Mile End Park

Mile End Park is a kilometre of modern parkland that uses the canal as its western boundary. The space is divided into sections – art, ecology, sport and wildlife *(see previous page)*. Though planned in the 1940s, it was never fully realised until 2000. From the air, this part of the Mile End Park looks like a decorative leaf. Parts of the park have become sadly neglected since its inception but it is still worth deviating off the towpath at this point to view the gardens.

Mile End Underground

5 King George's Field

Originally set up as one of 471 recreational areas established as a memorial to King George V who died in 1936. This sports facility south of Mile End Park contains a running track, a football pitch and numerous all-weather training areas, plus a swimming pool, gym and a sports hall.

Regent's Canal

Johnson's Lock

Mile End Road

2 Queen's Building/New People's Palace

Located on Mile End Road to the west of the canal, the imposing and ornate Queen's Building *(below right)* is set back off the road. It is the focal point of Queen Mary University but was formerly the People's Palace until a fire in 1931 damaged it. Six years later a new People's Palace was built immediately next door. This multi-purpose building *(below left)* was used for meetings, theatre, arts, sport and dance. It features external reliefs by Eric Gill *(left)*. It is now part of the University.

4 Stepney Blitz Memorial

Just off Candle Street are four black metal structures set in an arc. These are all that now remain of the gasometers that stood on this site. By the canal is a memorial to the firewatchers who saved the gasometers from enemy bombing.

Cand

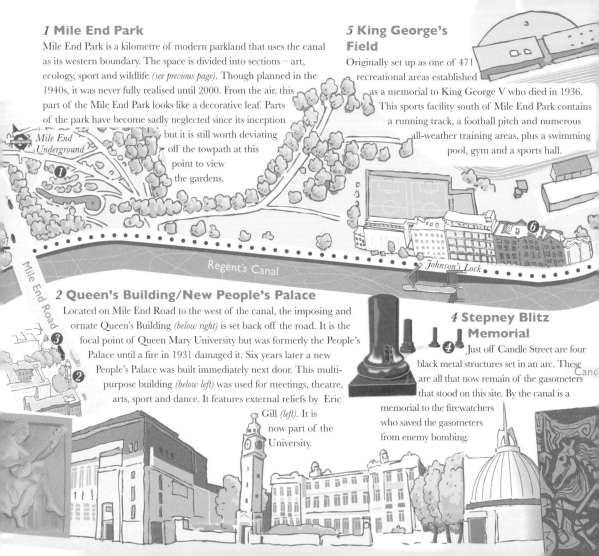

MILE END PARK

This is a very diverse section of the canal: the greenery of Mile End Park continues along the eastern bank; there are numerous pieces of industrial archeology that can be found along with public art by Eric Gill and a museum to East End Victorian school life.

This solitary chimney is a ventilation shaft for a sewage pipe, c.1906.

△ *Southend | Fenchurch Street* △

6 The Ragged School Museum

This museum is set in the warehouses that Dr Thomas Barnardo (1845–1905), in 1876, converted into the 'Ragged School'. Barnardo was alarmed at the number of children he found begging and sleeping rough in east London. Over the next thirty years the Ragged School provided shelter for children of the area.

Barnardo went on to establish care homes for vunerable and neglected children across the UK. The warehouse, in Copperfield Road, has been saved from demolition and is now a museum of Victorian school life.

Dr Barnardo's

Salmon Lane Lock

Salmon Lane

7 Back pumping

The supply of water to the canal became critical as the Regent's Canal became more successful in the nineteenth century. Each lowering or raising of a lock used over 200,000 litres of water. So a series of back pumping stations were created to pump water up from the Limehouse Basin to Camden. North of Commercial Road, set into the embankment, off the towpath, is an isolator valve.

⑦

Commercial Road

3 St Benet's Chaplaincy

In what appears be a small astronomical observatory is a circular chapel with a domed roof, called St Benet's. Built in 1964, the interior of the chapel features Romanesque style sgraffito murals *(left)* by the Polish-born artist Adam Kossowski.

Limehouse
DLR

LIMEHOUSE

Commercial Road – Limehouse Cut entrance 365m

Coal had been imported from the north-east of England into Limehouse from the thirteenth until the twentieth century. The name Limehouse was derived from the lime kilns established in the area in the fourteenth century to manufacture quicklime for building mortar. It was around this time that shipbuilding began here on the north bank of the River Thames.

By the eighteenth century, many foreign casual sailors, once paid off, chose to live in Limehouse. The first London Chinatown was established by Han Chinese sailors.

The Limehouse Basin is now the hub for three major London waterways: the River Thames, the Regent's Canal and the Limehouse Cut. During the nineteenth century it became the gateway to Britain's canal network.

Right: Hydraulic cranes that once operated in the Basin

Limehouse DLR

1 Limehouse Basin

This was formerly known as Regent's Canal Dock and was built by the Regent's Canal Company in 1820 to connect the canal with the River Thames. It was the point where seagoing vessels loaded and unloaded cargo on to the canal barges and narrowboats.

Due to the success of the Dock, it had to expand several times to improve the handling capacity. Wharf buildings and bonded warehouses surrounded the quayside. At its peak the water covered more than 4 hectares, but with the decline in canal traffic it ceased being a commercial operation in 1969 and the cranes *(left)* were removed.

During the 1980s a whole swathe of the declining London docks, including the basin, were redeveloped as office, residential and shopping areas. Many of the old warehouses and buildings were demolished to make way for the structures that are present today.

The Limehouse Basin is now a modern marina for 90 boats – river, seagoing and narrowboats. It is surrounded by 'desirable' apartments and offices. There is a road tunnel, the Limehouse Link, that runs immediately below the basin. It connects the City to Canary Wharf.

Route down to the River Thames 630m >

N

Righ Harbe Maste offic

S

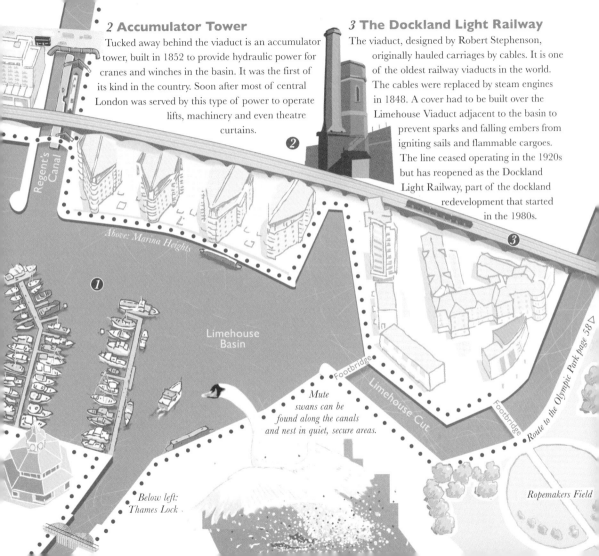

2 Accumulator Tower

Tucked away behind the viaduct is an accumulator tower, built in 1852 to provide hydraulic power for cranes and winches in the basin. It was the first of its kind in the country. Soon after most of central London was served by this type of power to operate lifts, machinery and even theatre curtains.

②

3 The Dockland Light Railway

The viaduct, designed by Robert Stephenson, originally hauled carriages by cables. It is one of the oldest railway viaducts in the world. The cables were replaced by steam engines in 1848. A cover had to be built over the Limehouse Viaduct adjacent to the basin to prevent sparks and falling embers from igniting sails and flammable cargoes. The line ceased operating in the 1920s but has reopened as the Dockland Light Railway, part of the dockland redevelopment that started in the 1980s.

③

Regent's Canal

Above: Marina Heights

①

Limehouse Basin

Footbridge

Limehouse Cut

Footbridge

Route to the Olympic Park page 58 ▷

Mute swans can be found along the canals and nest in quiet, secure areas.

Below left: Thames Lock

Ropemakers Field

1 The Grapes

A public house has stood on this site at 76 Narrow Street since 1583. It featured in *Our Mutual Friend* by Charles Dickens, 'A tavern of dropsical appearance . . . long settled down into a state of hale infirmity'. Beer was originally supplied from the Taylor Walker brewery that used to stand opposite the pub. It is currently owned by Evgeny Lebedev (proprietor of the *Evening Standard*), theatre director Sean Mathias and actor Sir Ian McKellen.

Above:
Canary Wharf

2 Limehouse Cut Entrance

The Thames entrance to the Limehouse Cut was dammed-up in 1968 following its re-connection to the Limehouse Basin. The remains of this canal prior to the Thames is now merely decorative.

Narrow Street

Dickens and Limehouse

Charles Dickens visited Limehouse from a very early age, as his godfather, a sail maker, lived in the area. The area was then vastly different from the Limehouse of today. It was a run down, slum district with a diverse population that relied upon the river for employment. London's first outbreak of cholera in 1832 was in Limehouse. It was here that Dickens would locate many of his fictional characters: The shipping company of Dombey and Son was based in Narrow Street, John Jasper from *The Mystery of Edwin Drood* visited the Limehouse opium dens and The Grapes of Narrow Street featured in *Our Mutual Friend*.

THE THAMES

The Regent's Canal and the River Thames finally meet. The panoramic views from this intersection, of Canary Wharf, the City and The Shard are worth a detour off the towpath. This area of Limehouse that rubs up against the Thames has been a popular haunt of writers and artists. Whistler created his 'nocturne' of Limehouse here and Francis Bacon lived at 80 Narrow Street. Many writers' characters visited this location: Oscar Wilde's *Dorian Grey*, Arthur Conan Doyle's *Sherlock Holmes* and Peter Ackroyd's *Dan Leno and Limehouse Golem*.

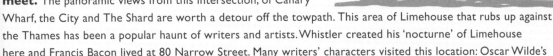

4 The Bread Basket

This building was originally the customs and harbour master's office. It is now a Gordon Ramsey restaurant called The Bread Basket, located right by the mouth of the Thames Lock at 44 Narrow Street. It was originally called the Barley Mow. The riverside tables command great views of the Thames, the shoreline architecture and beyond.

Narrow Street

3 The Thames Lock

Following the closure of the Limehouse Basin to commercial sea-going traffic in the late 1960s, a much smaller lock was needed. The old Ship Lock was filled in and replaced with the Thames Lock, which uses 90 per cent less water. Unlike every other lock on the Regent's Canal, this one is still operated by lock keepers.

5 Sir David Lean 1908–91

The British film director lived at number 30 Narrow Street (Sun Wharf) until his death. He directed many great films including *Dr Zhivago*, *Brief Encounter* and *Lawrence of Arabia*, plus several adaptations of Dickens' novels *(right)*.

LIMEHOUSE CUT

Once around the initial two bends of the Limehouse Cut, the open spaces of the marina are left behind and we are back on to a long straight canal strip, bordered with a large assortment of recently built and converted residential apartments. These are slowly replacing the unprepossessing array of decayed warehouses and factories that stood by the canal. When the cut was opened in 1770 it attracted the more odorous industries such as potash, lime and chemical manufacturers. It was locally known as 'stinkinghouse'. This reputation has not fully been shaken off, but just off the towpath are some redeeming features.

1 The Mission

This imposing art deco edifice on Commercial Road, built in 1924, was once the Empire Memorial Sailors' Hostel. It has been converted into apartments.

2 St Anne's Church

This fine example of restrained baroque design was created by Nicholas Hawksmoor (1661–1736) and built between 1714 and 1725 though not consecrated until 1730. This is one of three East End churches that Hawksmoor designed, including Christ Church, Spitalfields. Hawksmoor was originally a clerk to Sir Christopher Wren (architect of St Paul's cathedral). The west bell tower is visible for miles and was used by sailors on the Thames as a navigational beacon. The interior was gutted by fire in 1851 but was faithfully restored. The church is located just off Newell Street.

The Ropemakers of Limehouse

Limehouse became famous for the quality of rope it produced for nautical use. Sisal fibre was spun into rope between two rigid wooden frames. These frames, known as *ropewalks* could be several hundred metres apart.

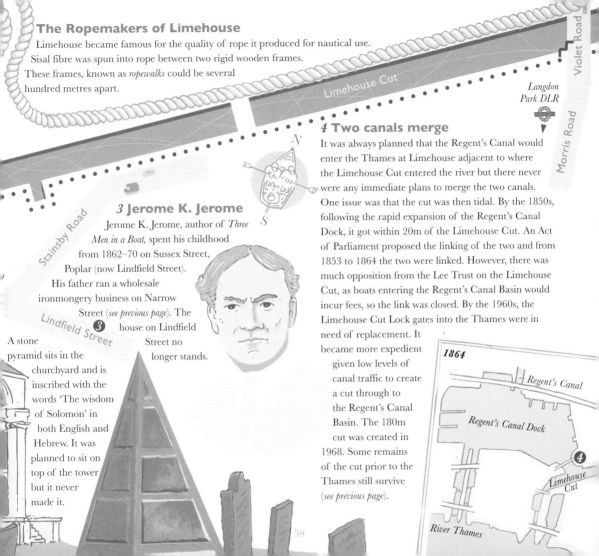

3 Jerome K. Jerome

Jerome K. Jerome, author of *Three Men in a Boat,* spent his childhood from 1862–70 on Sussex Street, Poplar (now Lindfield Street). His father ran a wholesale ironmongery business on Narrow Street (*see previous page*). The house on Lindfield Street no longer stands.

A stone pyramid sits in the churchyard and is inscribed with the words 'The wisdom of Solomon' in both English and Hebrew. It was planned to sit on top of the tower but it never made it.

4 Two canals merge

It was always planned that the Regent's Canal would enter the Thames at Limehouse adjacent to where the Limehouse Cut entered the river but there never were any immediate plans to merge the two canals. One issue was that the cut was then tidal. By the 1850s, following the rapid expansion of the Regent's Canal Dock, it got within 20m of the Limehouse Cut. An Act of Parliament proposed the linking of the two and from 1853 to 1864 the two were linked. However, there was much opposition from the Lee Trust on the Limehouse Cut, as boats entering the Regent's Canal Basin would incur fees, so the link was closed. By the 1960s, the Limehouse Cut Lock gates into the Thames were in need of replacement. It became more expedient given low levels of canal traffic to create a cut through to the Regent's Canal Basin. The 180m cut was created in 1968. Some remains of the cut prior to the Thames still survive (*see previous page*).

1864

Regent's Canal

Regent's Canal Dock

Limehouse Cut

River Thames

Langdon Park DLR

BOW LOCKS

Violet Road Bridge – District Line Bridge 1,080m

The Short Cut

City of London

River Thames

The towpath and canal continue their arrow straight course towards the A12 dual carriageway and Bow Locks beyond. Immediately after Violet Road Bridge is the former Spratts Dog Biscuit factory, with its preserved exterior signage.

Despite Bow Locks' proximity to the dual carriageway, there is quite a change in atmosphere here. The waterways of the Limehouse Cut / River Lee Navigation and the Bow Creek are linked but due to the tides, the variation in water levels can be very dramatic. The sense of space suddenly increases here and the vista dramatically improves.

Dangerous structure Keep out

Violet Road

Limehouse Cut

❶

❷

Langdon Park DLR

Morris Road

1 Spratts Dog Biscuit Factory

An American, James Spratt, created the first patented dog biscuit in the 1860s in London. The dog biscuit factory, on the south side of the Limehouse Cut by Morris Road, was opened in the late 1890s and became the largest of its type in the world. The canal was used to import the raw materials: beetroot, vegetables, wheat and meat, for the 'meat fibrine dog cakes' and to export the finished products. The factory went on to produce many different types of animal feed. Though the company has long gone the terrier logo *(below)* is still visible along with the signage. The factory building still stands, though it has been converted into studio workshops. It is best viewed from the Violet Road Bridge.

❸

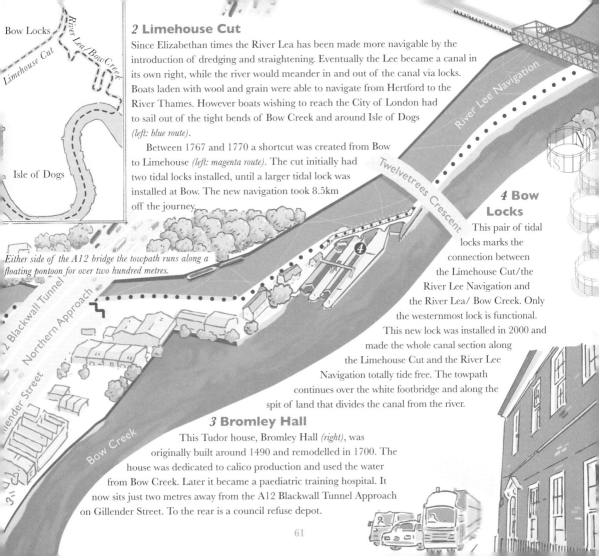

2 Limehouse Cut

Since Elizabethan times the River Lea has been made more navigable by the introduction of dredging and straightening. Eventually the Lee became a canal in its own right, while the river would meander in and out of the canal via locks. Boats laden with wool and grain were able to navigate from Hertford to the River Thames. However boats wishing to reach the City of London had to sail out of the tight bends of Bow Creek and around Isle of Dogs *(left: blue route)*.

Between 1767 and 1770 a shortcut was created from Bow to Limehouse *(left: magenta route)*. The cut initially had two tidal locks installed, until a larger tidal lock was installed at Bow. The new navigation took 8.5km off the journey.

Bow Locks

River Lea/Bow Creek

Limehouse Cut

Isle of Dogs

Either side of the A12 bridge the towpath runs along a floating pontoon for over two hundred metres.

River Lee Navigation

Twelvetrees Crescent

4 Bow Locks

This pair of tidal locks marks the connection between the Limehouse Cut/the River Lee Navigation and the River Lea/ Bow Creek. Only the westernmost lock is functional. This new lock was installed in 2000 and made the whole canal section along the Limehouse Cut and the River Lee Navigation totally tide free. The towpath continues over the white footbridge and along the spit of land that divides the canal from the river.

Blackwall Tunnel Northern Approach

ender Street

Bow Creek

3 Bromley Hall

This Tudor house, Bromley Hall *(right)*, was originally built around 1490 and remodelled in 1700. The house was dedicated to calico production and used the water from Bow Creek. Later it became a paediatric training hospital. It now sits just two metres away from the A12 Blackwall Tunnel Approach on Gillender Street. To the rear is a council refuse depot.

LOST THEIR LIVES   A WEI
THE FIRST NAMED WHILE II
OVERCOME BY FOUL AII
NG IN HEROIC EFFO
GODERLY MAULE N
·R THREE W!

2 3 Mills Studios

This is a large TV, film and music production space. Films including *Fantastic Mr Fox*, *Sherlock Holmes: A Game of Shadows*, *Sunshine* and *The Reader* were all made here.

River Lee Navigation

Three Mills Wall River

House Mill

1 The House and Clock Mills

The original medieval tidal mill was bought by three Huguenots in 1727 for the propose of distilling gin and grinding flour. The ebb (outgoing) tide would drive the four paddle wheels. These in turn would drive twelve pairs of mill stones. This process continued until halted by German aerial bombing in 1941. The House Mill *(above left)* is now a Grade I listed building and it is believed to be the largest tidal mill still in existence in the world. The charitable trust that runs the mill is hoping to start generating hydro-electricity using two of the paddle wheels. Adjacent to the Mill House is the Clock Mill, built in 1753, containing two drying kilns (oast roofs).

Three Mills Lane

Clock Mill

Bromley-by-Bow

Bow Creek

3 Three Mills Green memorial

This replacement memorial was erected in 2002 to four men who were killed by toxic gases in a nearby well in 1901. It is worth detouring to this point to view the Abbey Mills Pumping Station.

4 Three Mills Lock

The lock, opened in 2009, was built as part of the Olympic Park development, to give construction barges access to and from the Thames and also reduce the risk of flooding.

5 Abbey Mills Pumping Station

From Three Mills Green the Abbey Mills Pumping Station on Abbey Lane can be seen to the east. This superb piece of Venetian gothic has been described as a 'cathedral of sewage'. It was created by the engineer Sir Joseph Bazalgette in 1868 and was designed to pump effluent into the northern outfall pipe. It originally had two Byzantine-style chimneys adjacent to the structure but these were removed for safety during the Second World War. The eight steam engine pumps were decommissioned in the 1930s and replaced with electric ones. The building and its interior can be viewed on certain days of the year. The aluminium structure *(right)* is the pumping station's replacement.

Prescott Channel

Channelsea River

THREE MILLS

District Line Bridge – Bow Road / A12 intersection 1,155m (including the Memorial diversion)

The towpath continues along what is a long thin island, with the River Lee Navigation to the west and Bow Creek to the east. Three Mills is sited on an ancient man-made island, between the River Lee Navigation and the Bow Back Rivers. It is an almost rural oasis away from the east London sprawl that surrounds it. There has been a mill on this site since before the Domesday Book. It is sited on the old border between the counties of Middlesex and Essex.

Just to the east of Three Mills is the Abbey Mills Pumping Station, a jewel of Victorian architecture.

The new pumping station

Weathervane from the Clock Mill

1 St Mary, Bow

This 700-year-old church sits isolated on an island in the middle of Bow Road. Many parts of the church have been rebuilt or replaced over the centuries due to neglect or bomb damage. During the English Reformation, the church was under the control of Bishop Bonner *(see page 46)*. Many heretics were burnt at the stake in front of the church.

Fairfield Road

2 Bryant & May Factory

This match factory was founded at Bow in 1860 and was the scene of the matchgirls' strike in 1888. The strikers campaigned against the use of the potentially fatal white phosphorous in the manufacture of matches which could result in jaw disease (phossy jaw). The strikers, with the assistance of the women's rights activist, Annie Bessant, won and established safer working conditions within the factory. The factory was rebuilt in 1911 *(above)* and could produce over 10,000 million matches per year with the much safer red phosphorous. The factory closed in 1979 and has since been converted into residential apartments.

Above: A carved detail above the porter's lodge entrance on Fairfield Road. It is one of several with nautical motifs to be found on the former match factory.

Right: Once beyond the Bow Road/A12 intersection, the London Stadium becomes visible over the factory and warehouse roofs.

Bow Road A11

Lee Navigation

A12

PROTECTION FROM FIRE.
BRYANT & MAY'S
PATENT
SPECIAL SAFETY MATCH
IS NOT POISONOUS

3 Greenway

The Greenway is a footpath and cycleway built on top of a main sewer pipe (see next page).

4 Old Ford Lock

The lock marks the start of the Hackney Cut to the north. It was created in 1769, as a further development of the Lee Navigation but this location is probably best known as the location for Channel 4's *Big Breakfast*. For twenty years from 1992 the show was broadcast from the old lock keeper's house. It had a much lighter presentation style than many of its rivals. TV-am, also based by the canal in Camden, closed several months after *Big Breakfast* started.

5 Fish Island

The so-called 'island' is bounded by the Hertford Union Canal, Lee Navigation and the Greenway to the south. It is named after a set of streets with freshwater piscatorial street names – Dace, Bream and Roach – and the boundary on the A12 is marked with decorative fin shaped pennants. It is also home to H. Foreman, producers of smoked salmon. Dotted among the warehouses and factories are numerous artists' studios.

BREAM STREET E.3

Hertford Union Canal: see page 48
Left: Top Lock

Canal fish: Roach

RIVER LEE NAVIGATION

Bow Road / A12 intersection – White Post Lane Bridge 1,760m

The Lee Navigation is a canalised section of the River Lea that runs from Hereford to the River Thames. South of the Hackney Cut the navigation splits into several channels to form a man-made water complex known as the Bow Back Rivers. These were created largely by medieval monks, who drained the marshes and increased the water supply to the local mills. The Navigation played a vital part in the construction of the Olympic Park, as development and dredging in the early 2000s allowed 350-ton barges to carry materials in and refuse away from the site.

QUEEN ELIZABETH OLYMPIC

This area of London's East End wasteland was chosen in 2006 to be the focal point of the 2012 Olympic Games. The whole area underwent a massive redevelopment and regeneration; the industrial landscape was flattened, and rivers blocked and diverted. To the south runs the Victorian Northern Outfall Sewer. Above this huge raised pipework runs the Greenway, a walk and cycleway. It is worth a detour off the towpath on to this trail to view the Queen Elizabeth Olympic Park. At over 100 hectares it is now one of the largest urban parks in Europe.

②

1 Northern Outfall Sewer

Following a major outbreak of cholera in London in 1858, a major engineering scheme was established to improve the sewage system. Sir Joseph Bazalgette, the chief engineer of London's Metropolitan Board of Works, proposed a series of sewerage networks across London. The Northern Outfall Sewer feeds down into the processing plant at Beckton. During the Second World War defensive pillboxes were installed to defend against possible invasion *(below left)*. The footpath along the top of the pipes, the Greenway, forms part of the Capital Ring walking route.

2 The London Stadium

The stadium was built on a former industrial site within the man-made complex of the Bow Back Rivers and was designed by the architectural company Populous. It has none of the pizzazz of the Beijing Olympic Bird's Nest stadium; however, part of the brief was that the stadium should be sustainable and could be rescaled for other sporting uses once the games had finished, and not left to decay as other Olympic stadia have done. West Ham Football Club now have residency of the stadium and the capacity has been reduced down from 80,000 to 60,000 for football games. Athletic and concerts also take place within the arena.

Lee Navigation

Hackney Wick

Greenway

①

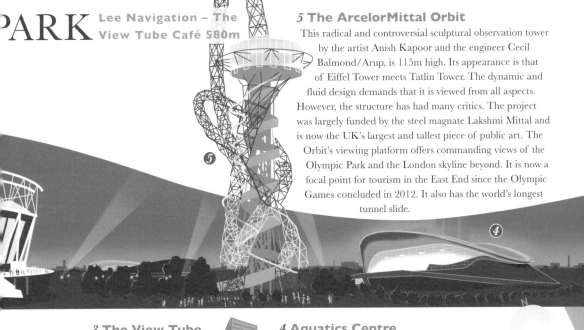

5 The ArcelorMittal Orbit

This radical and controversial sculptural observation tower by the artist Anish Kapoor and the engineer Cecil Balmond/Arup, is 115m high. Its appearance is that of Eiffel Tower meets Tatlin Tower. The dynamic and fluid design demands that it is viewed from all aspects. However, the structure has had many critics. The project was largely funded by the steel magnate Lakshmi Mittal and is now the UK's largest and tallest piece of public art. The Orbit's viewing platform offers commanding views of the Olympic Park and the London skyline beyond. It is now a focal point for tourism in the East End since the Olympic Games concluded in 2012. It also has the world's longest tunnel slide.

3 The View Tube

The café *(right)* and open-sided art gallery are constructed from recycled shipping containers. They are located about 600m from the Lee Navigation and provide a good stopping off point to view the Queen Elizabeth Olympic Park.

4 Aquatics Centre

Designed by Zaha Hadid, this 160m parabolic arched structure represents 'the fluid geometry of water in motion'. Of all the 2012 Olympic stadia, this is probably the most stunning and elegant. During the Games it seated 17,500 people through the use of two temporary wings. These were removed after the Games to reveal the true dynamics of the centre. It now has a capacity of 2,500.

ACKNOWLEDGEMENTS

My thanks to the following: Chris Dane for the Two Stadium cycling tour (it kindled this book into existence) and for his proofreading of the initial pages, Sheila Fathers for her time and dedication checking the proofs, Chrissie Charlton, Monika Day, Jeremy Nicholas of the Jerome K. Jerome Society, Revd Jenny Peterson of St Benet's, chaplain to the Queen Mary, University of London, Ian Shacklock, of the Friends of the Regent's Canal, Alex Szyszkowski and the late Philip Walker of jewisheastend.com.

WEB LINKS

Robert Browning	*browningsociety.org*
Camden Lock	*camdenmarket.com*
The London Canal Museum	*canalmuseum.org.uk*
Camley Street Natural Park	*wildlondon.org.uk*
Central Mosque of London	*iccuk.org*
Friends of the Regent's Canal	*friendsofregentscanal.org*
The Jewish East End	*jewisheastend.com*
King's Cross development	*kingscrosscentral.com*
Kings Place	*kingsplace.co.uk*
The London Water Bus	*londonwaterbus.com*
London Zoo	*zsl.org*
Lord's Cricket Ground	*lords.org*
St Pancras Cruising Club	*stpancrascc.co.uk*
The Pirate Castle	*thepiratecastle.org*
The Puppet Barge	*puppetbarge.com*
Q & F Terry Architects	*qftarchitects.com*
The Ragged School Museum	*raggedschoolmuseum.org.uk*
The Three Mills	*housemill.org.uk*
Victoria Park	*victoriaparkvillage.com*
The View Tube	*theviewtube.co.uk*
Word on the Water	*wordonthewater.co.uk*
Zaha Hadid Architects	*zaha-hadid.com*

BIBLIOGRAPHY

Author(s)	Title	Publisher	Year
Ackroyd, Peter	Dickens	Vintage	2002
Cameron-Cooper, Gilly	Walking London's Docks, River and Canals	New Holland	2005
Cherry, Bridget & Pevsner, Nikolaus	The Buildings of England London 3: North West	Penguin	1999
Cherry, Bridget & Pevsner, Nikolaus	The Buildings of England London 4: North	Yale University Press	2002
Cherry, Bridget; O'Brien, Charles & Pevsner, Nikolaus	The Buildings of England London 5: East	Yale University Press	2005
Essex- Lopresti, Michael	Exploring the Regent's Canal	Brewin Books	2000
Faulkner, Alan	The Regent's Canal	Waterways World	2005
Hyde, Ralph	The A–Z of Victorian London	Harry Margary	1987
Jones, Edward & Woodward, Christopher	A Guide to the Architecture of London	Weidenfeld & Nicolas	1983
Meeks, Carroll L.V.	The Railroad Station	Castle Books	1978
Montefiore, Simon Sebag	Young Stalin	Weidenfeld & Nicolas	2007
Mosley, Charlotte	The Letters of Nancy Mitford	Sceptre	1994
Philpotts, Robert	When London Became an Island	Blackwater Books	2008
Ridge, T.S.	Dr Barnardo and the Copperfield Road Ragged School		1993
Spencer, Herbert	London's Canal	Putnam	1961
Talling, Paul	London's Lost Rivers	RH Books	2011
Tench, Richard & Hillman, Ellis	London Under London	John Murray	1994

Maps

Author(s)	Title	Publisher	Year
Bacon	A Street Map of London 1843	Old House Books	
Bacon	Bacon's New Map of London 1902	Old House Books	
Dean, Richard	Canals of London	Richard Dean	1996
Cruchley	New Plan of London 1839 (reprint)	Tower Hamlets Library	1998
Laurie and Whittle	New Plan of London 1809–10 (reprint)	Tower Hamlets Library	2000
Laurie and Whittle	New Plan of London 1819 (reprint)	Tower Hamlets Library	1993
Old Ordnance Survey Maps	Stepney & Limehouse	Alan Godfrey Maps	1870
Old Ordnance Survey Maps	Stepney & Limehouse	Alan Godfrey Maps	1914
	Reference Atlas of Greater London	Bartholomew	1961

INDEX

Also by **David Fathers**

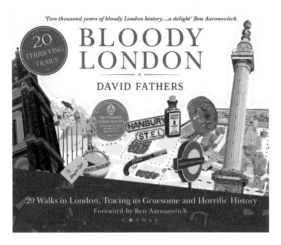

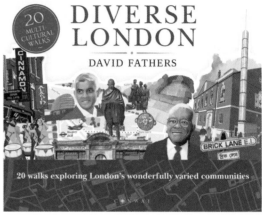

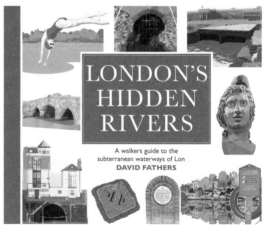